The Bluebird Flew Away

SHEILA MOONEY

POOLBEG

First published 1993 by
Poolbeg Press Ltd
Knocksedan House,
Swords, Co Dublin, Ireland

© Sheila Mooney 1993

The moral right of the author has been asserted.

A catalogue record for this book is available from the British Library.

ISBN 1 85371 255 8

Cover design by Pomphrey Associates
Set by Mac Book Limited in Stone 9.5/15
Printed by The Guernsey Press Company Ltd,
Vale, Guernsey, Channel Islands

My thanks to Jonathan Williams for his invaluable help, to my editor, Sean McMahon, and to Dr Alf Delaney for checking out the yachting research.

Also to all my friends in Poolbeg.

My family
Pauline, Billy, Wendy, and Oisin,
with all my love.

Here, traveller, scholar, poet, take your stand
When all those rooms and passages are gone,
When nettles wave upon a shapeless mound
And saplings root among the broken stone...

"Coole Park, 1929"

WB Yeats

Contents

1

A SUMMER GIRLHOOD

I believe the past is always with us; as with dead friends and relations, it lives in the heart. The gracious living, the glittering hospitality of the big houses, the gladness, the sadness, good conversation like vintage wine, has made me part of what I am. Before I tell of my new kind of living, I shall indulge myself in remembering.

In the mid-twenties and thirties summer holidays were spent at Annagh, the Frazer home of my grand-aunts, Kate and Anna. The house was near Boyle, in the county of Roscommon. The party of seven consisted of Mother, Aunt Mona, Mrs West—the tall gaunt wife of our gardener, Nannie and my two younger sisters. Nannie could not, or would not, control me, so Mrs West was my minder. And I hated her.

I loved those summer visits of my childhood. The old ivy-covered house was dusty and unkempt but it had a faded beauty, like the four-poster bed I used sleep in. This had a canopy and worn pink brocade curtains, tied back with gold cords rotting with age. There were shutters in the windows which were always latched at night to keep out the night air, which my aunts believed was unhealthy.

Aunt Kate was the efficient, bossy one. Mother said she had always been very plain. She supervised the running of the house and the garden. That too had run riot; everything grew undisturbed, enchanting for a child. To me it was like a jungle where one kept finding new paths leading to the river. Pink and white wild roses seemed to be everywhere.

Just inside the main gates the waterfall crashed down— all froth and foam; the brown water ran through the grounds and rose in the dappled woods a dark and mysterious lake. I used paddle and look for crayfish under the stones. My feet would get really cold and looked very white in the water. Sometimes I got afraid of them—they looked like little dead feet—and then I would jump out quickly and run up to the house.

There were three grand-aunts, the Misses Frazers, sisters of my late grandfather, my mother's father Dr John Frazer. These were known as the "aunts." The eldest, Lillah, died young of tuberculosis; Kate was the tough one and Anna the quiet one, always delicate, quite a famous artist. She attempted suicide when her fiancé was killed in a riding accident. My brother used to say, "She's amiably potty." I wondered what that was.

Uncle Harold, Mother's youngest brother, lived with the aunts. Mother used say he was a hanger-on; he was hoping to inherit their money. He even changed his religion and became Protestant because my grand-aunts did not like Catholics. He did nothing; he was a poet. He had bright blue eyes and looked sad. Father said Harold was a "damned waster" but I liked him; he told me lots of lovely things that I will never forget. He had heard the banshee, and he told me about the pookah that appeared at the crossroads, this—a big black dog—"unusually big"—was only seen when someone was going to die.

I was thrilled when Uncle Harold showed me the "will-o'-the-wisp" dancing on the bog; little twinkling lights that had to be fairies. Uncle Harold said they danced there so humans could not catch them. The bog was dangerous and, in some parts, "it could swallow you up."

Beatrice was the housekeeper at Annagh. She was very tall and had black hair and dark sparkling eyes. She used to say, "I have Spanish blood in my veins," and would dance and swirl round the kitchen. Aunt Kate said, "It would be a far better thing if Beatrice kept her mouth shut about the Spanish blood!" I asked Uncle Harold about this and he told me, "A long time ago a Spanish ship sailed into Lough Key, a good many girls 'fell by the way' and Beatrice's mother was one of them."

Well I did not understand a word of that, so I asked McConnell, the yard man, "Why has Beatrice to keep her mouth shut about her Spanish blood, and why did her mother fall by the way?" McConnell said, "Because, Miss, Beatrice is a bastard." He laughed. "She's an auld bastard and always will be!" I didn't know what a bastard was, but I said, "Her mother's fall; McConnell, tell me."

"That were no fall, Missie; she done it with yer Spanish man because she wanted to." Done it? Done what? The more I asked, the more muddlesome it got.

Beatrice let me come into her bedroom one day. There wasn't much in it. I had been in servants' rooms before. I knew they always got the old shabby stuff. There was a big cardboard box under her bed. "What's in the box under your bed?" I asked. She laughed. "It's me party outfit."

"But why do you keep it under the bed?"

"To be prepared to be ready in case I need it. It's my shroud, my laying-out clothes."

"I don't know what you mean," I said crossly.

"It's the clothes they will dress me in when I die. Everyone in the country keeps their laying-out clothes ready."

Beatrice showed me the clothes. They were horrible: a long brown thing with a hood called, she said, a "habit," a crucifix and a string of very long rosary beads. I felt very frightened and ran to find someone to "tell on her." I found Aunt Mona, who was very fond of children. "Don't mind her, darling," she said, "Beatrice is full of nonsense."

Beatrice did the cooking. Mother and Aunt Mona said she was a vile cook. Aunt Kate made the brown bread and on Saturday, for Sunday, she baked beautiful chocolate cakes. One day in the kitchen, I saw Beatrice looking in the spotty mirror. She had a black mole on her chin with hairs growing out of it. She was cutting the hairs and they fell into the rice pudding she was making. I said, "Beatrice, the hairs are in the pudding," but she only laughed.

At lunchtime the rice pudding was put on the table in front of Aunt Kate. She always served the portions.

I said, "None for me, Aunt Kate."

"Nonsense, child, it's nice."

What was I to do?

In a panic, I said, "There are three hairs off Beatrice's

chin in the pudding. I saw them fall in."

Uncle Harold jumped up and left the room. Mother and Aunt Mona were laughing. No one, not even the aunts, ate the pudding. Aunt Kate went to the kitchen and had a word with Beatrice. She said, "All right, all right. I'll give it to McConnell." He was greedy. I told him when he had scoffed up all the pudding. He looked very upset.

There was a maid called Mary, who stayed in the scullery, a dark room off the kitchen. Her jobs were peeling the potatoes, plucking the fowl, scouring the pots. She was allowed in the kitchen but not around the house. She always looked very tired and her apron was invariably dirty, but she was very pretty. I asked Beatrice why Mary wore a dirty apron. She said, "She is a slattern and a slut and no better than she should be." I told Uncle Harold and he said, "The big woman's jealous because Mary is a pretty girl." Poor Mary slept in the most awful place. There was an attic room in the scullery with four steps leading up to it. Once I climbed up to see it. There was a little window let into a slanting roof. The light showed a mattress with the ticking coming out, a dirty striped pillow and some torn blankets.

I heard a miaow! Sligo, the tortoise-shell cat, was in the corner sitting on a sack. She had four new kittens. I congratulated her, just as people did when Mother had her last baby: "Well done, I hope it wasn't too hard on you." I remembered not to touch the kittens. (When Sligo had her previous litter someone petted the kittens and she did a terrible thing: she ate two of them! I pretended to forgive her, but I never really did.) I told Aunt Kate, who became cross. "Mary belongs in the scullery and that's that. Keep away from the servants' quarters from now on." Uncle Harold was standing by and Aunt Kate said, "That could apply to you, Harold, and you know perfectly well what I mean." I did not know what she meant but Uncle Harold went very red and said "the old battle-axe" under his breath.

Poor Mary! Mother said the cat slept in the attic because they stored the potatoes there and sometimes rats would try to eat them.

2

PRIESTS AND MR POT-HAT

Twice a week McConnell used drive Beatrice in the pony and trap to Ballifarnon to stock up on groceries. Beatrice always used to say that she was going to visit her old mother but Uncle Harold said, "Old mother be damned; it's the pub and then a bit of how's your father." I did not understand. Uncle Harold said, "Time enough to understand the vagaries of this life," and then said what he always said when he started composing poems: "They multiplied star upon star." Father used to ask, "Who the hell were they?" and say that Harold Frazer was a damned fool, so I never asked who "they" were—but I wondered.

One hot summer's evening, Uncle Harold said to me, "Child, would you like to come to a wake, as part of your rural education?"

"What is a wake?"

"It's a party given by a dead person."

"How can a dead person give a party?"

"They don't, but before they die they ask their friends to arrange everything and, when they're gone, the friends give the party for the dead person."

"Will the dead person be at the party?"

"Oh yes, that's the whole point of it."

I felt scared and did not want to go. Mr Mulhall was the dead man's name; he was ninety-two and had died because, Uncle Harold said, "His number was up."

"Have we all got numbers then?"

"Yes, child, and when the number comes up, you have to go."

"Will my number come up? I don't want to go."

Uncle Harold laughed. "You're a sturdy little one. I don't think you'll be going for a long time."

"Where has Mr Mulhall gone? Has he gone up to heaven?"

"He'll be at the party but his spirit has gone to purgatory. Only Protestants go straight to heaven." Uncle Harold had just become a Protestant. Mother said he was playing up to the aunts; they were Protestants and they hated Catholics.

The wake was in a little cottage. The room was very dark and full of people; the only lights were candles in jam-jars. Some of the people sat on chairs while the rest stood. The women all had rosary beads and the men had glasses of black stuff called porter. The men stood back when we came in and some of them tipped their caps to Uncle Harold and said, "Good-night to you, Captain Frazer, and the little one." Then I saw it! I stood frozen to the ground in the middle of the room. Up on a table was a rough wooden coffin and in it was Mr Mulhall! I was terrified. He looked awful.

"Why is Mr Mulhall dressed up as a monk?"

"That is a shroud; better known as the brown habit."

The hood was pulled up over his head and he had brown pennies on his eyes.

"Why has he pennies on his eyes? Is that to pay his fare to purgatory?"

"It's to keep his eyes shut."

This was followed by: "If we took the pennies off, he could see the party."

"Child, he is better off not seeing the party."

Two very old women with black shawls over their heads knelt one on each side of the coffin. They were making an awful wailing noise—like the cats at night. Uncle Harold told me they were the keeners, who were called in to cry and mourn the dead.

"Why can't the others cry?"

"Because they are too drunk, child."

A fat woman came out of the kitchen with a big dish of crubeens, pigs' feet. They were disgusting. The fat woman was the widow Mulhall. She came over to us. "Thank you for coming, Captain Frazer; would the little angel like to pay her respects?"

She took me by the hand and—horrors—led me over to the coffin. There were four candles, two at the head and two at the bottom. They cast weird shadows on the ceiling and the two old women just went on and on wailing.

"Look at him, child. God rest him; he be a lovely corpse."

I glanced at him. He was so white and his mouth was all sucked in. To my horror, Mrs Mulhall put my hand on his forehead and it was cold and clammy. "A little prayer, pet, for the dead; 'twill bring a blessing on you."

Such an outing. Everyone was furious at Uncle Harold.

I had the light on all night. Nannie said, "That young one will be disturbed for a long time."

Aunt Mona was my mother's youngest sister. She was a bit deaf, but Mother said that if you mentioned money, she got her hearing back immediately! She had never got married but she loved children and was very good at telling stories. I was interested in an old hermit who lived up a boreen about a mile away from Annagh. Aunt Mona called him "little Mr Pot-hat." My great joy was for her to take me up the boreen to see Mr Pot-hat's home. It was a long stony walk. Cows wandered about; some stared at us and others kept their heads down chewing the grass and not bothering to look. I was not afraid of the creatures any more; they were gentle poor things.

Mr Pot-hat got his name because he always wore a beige hat with no brim. It looked like an upside-down flowerpot. He had no teeth and wore a dirty raincoat and black wellies. Beatrice said he had nothing on under his coat; Aunt Mona said, "Beatrice has a peculiar mind." He lived in a broken-down thatched cottage that had two rooms and an outside lavatory—a tall shed like a sentry box. Aunt Mona said, "He wouldn't need to be short taken during the winter." A white goat was chained to a post. Mr Pot-hat drank only goat's milk. He had nailed up sacks as curtains in the two windows. There was no glass. Beatrice said it was a "pigsty inside." Sometimes Mr Pot-hat pulled the sack aside and peered out. That was really exciting and we would run away screaming. They said in the village that he had once been a lord but that, when his wife killed herself, he went mad.

The village children would sometimes come up and stone his house. I felt sorry for him. Aunt Mona made up a verse about him:

> Little Mr Pot-hat looking for a bride,
> Saw her up a back lane,
> Said, "Jump on my backside!"

I later recited it for the archdeacon when he called, and he dropped his teacup. Aunt Kate sent me out of the room.

On Sundays the aunts went to service in the local church. A vintage taxi called for them. They wore long dresses and motoring bonnets with veils over their face to keep off the dust. There was a big horn on the driver's side that he honked as they drove off. Aunt Kate said they drove at twenty-five miles an hour and poor Aunt Anna was really very nervous.

I was a Catholic child, and the only other Catholic was Beatrice; so she had to take me to mass in St Columcille's. It was a small church with beautiful coloured windows with angels on them. Some of the statues looked like dolls with rosy cheeks and red lips. Two of them, Holy Mary and Saint Anthony, had red lamps burning in front of them and vases with bunches of dusty artificial flowers. Mother said the parish was poor and they had no money to make the church nice. There were four confession boxes, two on each side of the aisle. The shiny upright benches had hard boards for kneeling. Beatrice said, "Your knees are meant to hurt. It's for penance for your sins."

In the nineteen twenties and thirties Catholics normally

went to confession before receiving Holy Communion and had to fast from the previous midnight. I used to hear lots of tummies rumbling at those early masses! Beatrice, Mary and I had to get up at seven (in the dark in winter) to reach the church for eight o'clock mass. McConnell took us in the pony and trap. He drove very fast and we bumped along the stony road in the grey dawn. I hated the way he hit Murphy the pony with the whip to hurry him up. Usually when we got to the church, it was nearly full and some of the people had walked miles to get there. One side was for men and the other for women. The mass was in Latin and very boring, except when the priest opened the tabernacle, the little house on the altar where Jesus lives. I could never see the inside but I always wondered if it was like a beautiful doll's house.

Aunt Mona told me there were special weddings for "fallen girls" who were getting married with babies in their tummies. They were married outside the altar rails and could not wear white. This was to show their disgrace. Aunt Mona said decent girls did not have babies unless they were married.

There was always a long queue outside Father Turley's confession box. McConnell said it was because he was deaf and could not hear a bloody word. Mother said there was no point in going in. Still, I hoped that when I made my first confession, the priest would be deaf.

Then there was the ceremony of "churching." When a woman had given birth to a little baby, she had to go and be prayed over, because she had carried an unbaptised child with "original sin on its soul" in her stomach. The baby is cleansed of sin through baptism. Mother said, "It's the fathers who should be 'churched.' It's their damned fault." I didn't understand any of it but I was glad when Uncle Harold told me, "It's all damned nonsense. Little babies are little angels and if they die they go to heaven and not some limbo place the church made up."

The priests in the country were very highly thought of, largely because they were the ones with education. On duty, they wore long black coats called soutanes, and on their heads really funny little hats called birettas which had pom-poms on top.

Because I was the one in the middle—with two grown up and two in the nursery—I was like an only child. The house and grounds at Annagh were fairytale places for me. I loved to sit by the waterfall but I hardly ever went down to the dark woods where the lake rose. The only light was eerie dappled sunlight and the tall trees were full of black crows that called to each other with strange voices. I was afraid I might see the ghost of Aunt Edith, who had drowned herself there. The country people said at night she had been seen running crazy through the woods, wet hair tangled with green weed. I thought of Camelot, "many-towered Camelot," and the Lady of Shalott. Uncle Harold told me that when they took Aunt Edith's body from the river he had thought of the lady too, "especially when I looked at her face." He said he had quoted, "'...she has a lovely face;/God in his mercy lend her grace.'" The Frazers were an unlucky family; they believed a curse had been put upon them. Hence again:

Out flew the web and floated wide;
The mirror crack'd from side to side;
"The curse has come upon me" cried
The Lady of Shalott.

I hope she rests in peace.

I was always fond of writing and when I was seven I
wrote this little poem for Uncle Harold.

In the Heart of a Child

I think of a place in the heart of a child
Where the brown waters sparkle and flow.
Time like the river flows on
And the old people they have to go.
The house is so old and
The garden's grown wild.
These thoughts are all locked
In the heart of a child.

3

THE LAST OF THE FRAZERS

Some unthinking city folk say country people are thick but this is patently absurd. They have the knowledge of old ways, know herbal remedies and, like foxes, have their ear to the ground. There were some memorable characters in the district such as Biddy Broderick. She had a humped back and used to wander about always followed by a procession of dogs. Beatrice said she had never washed, so her skin was quite black. One day she said Biddy had given birth to a litter of collie pups. I said, "Oh please, please, take me to see them."

Biddy wore two coats and boots with no laces, and always had a shawl about her head. She lived in Ballinafad in a dirty and dilapidated cottage. I was afraid and said, "I don't want to go in," but Beatrice shoved me in ahead of her. There was a dark kitchen with a room off it.

"Who be there?" an old voice called out.

I shivered. Beatrice said, "Hallo there, Biddy. I've brought a wee girl to see you and the pups."

"Come in then; come in to be sure."

In the middle of the room was a huge bed and she sat

up in it amid a mess of tattered rags and rugs. At first I could not see anything in the dim light but eventually I could make out six little black-and-white puppies, all snuggled up together. The smell in the room was so bad, I could not take much interest.

"How's the pups then, Bid?" said Beatrice.

"Doing well, doing well. It's no trouble having them."

"How's the father? Is he pleased?"

"Of course he's pleased."

She looked at me. "Look out the window, child, and you'll see himself chasing the chickens. He'll be up later to see us all." *He* was a big collie dog and he was barking and chasing his tail. I suppose he was delighted with the new family.

Mrs West did not approve of such adventures. "You should report all these things to the Major [my father] when we get home," she said to Nannie. "The nonsense this child has been told. The country isn't good for her; she'll be harder to manage than before." McConnell said when I told him, "The sour old bat. You enjoy your life, missie, and take no heed—no heed at all." For once I liked him.

Aunt Kate told me many stories about her life and that of her sisters when they were girls. She always started the stories by saying, "Once upon a time, long, long ago." There had been three Miss Frazers, grandfather Frazer's sisters (he being my mother's father). Lillah, the eldest one, died very young of tuberculosis. Aunt Anna was the only beautiful one. There was an oil-painting of her in a white ball gown done when she was eighteen; I never would have guessed it was of the same person. She used sing and play the piano. Her fiancé had been killed in a hunting accident and after that she never sang again. I wondered about her. When I was six I sang "Just a Song at Twilight" for her and I saw a tear run down her face.

It seemed that their social life as girls was never dull. They were well-off, which helped in every respect. In the summer at Annagh, Corodoo, Riversdale, Kilronan and Hollybrook House—the big houses owned by ascendancy families, most of them related to the Frazers—all the people joined together to have picnics at the caves at Givah, Bally-farnon or on the beaches of Sligo. People from as many as thirty families, old and young alike, would gather for the outings. I have seen old sepia photographs with the ladies in their long dresses and parasols and the gentlemen in blazers and straw boaters. The little girls wore *broderie anglaise* dresses and black stockings and had coloured ribbons in their long hair. In those days a girl did not put up her hair until she came out at eighteen. The little boys wore sailor-suits and the older ones knickerbockers and caps.

Even the gundogs went. The Annagh dogs were picturesquely named: Grouse, Shot, Bloomer and Snipe! The gillies, or yard men, drove the pony traps and minded the dogs, and the nannies took care of the children. There seemed to be so many "minders" in those days; the aunts even had a ladies' maid to help them dress and to style their hair. The teas were sumptuous: the ladies had baked beautiful cakes and scones and prepared cucumber-and-watercress sandwiches.

According to Aunt Kate, journeys to the city were made in barges that were drawn by great horses. Every night the travellers stopped at one of the many little towns along the canal and were entertained at the big houses. One of them was the home of their brother, Dr John Frazer, who lived at Riversdale, about a quarter of a mile from Lough Key. This was a large and beautiful Tudor-style mansion, where my mother, her brothers and sisters lived after they had to leave Tientsin in 1900 because of the Boxer Rebellion. The canal journey from Boyle to Dublin took ten days!

I had some not-so-nice memories too. I remember hearing screams from the kitchen at Annagh. Mary, the kitchen maid, was standing on the table, Beatrice had her apron over her face, McConnell was laughing loudly, and a brown and headless hen was running round flapping its wings. McConnell was holding the head in his bloody hands. He was a cruel man. Uncle Harold said he enjoyed killing the pigs. I used hear them squealing as he cut their throats with a knife.

There's an old saying in the country that the man who made time made lots of it. In Roscommon we were very conscious of the past. One of the interesting features was the crannogs, funny humpy things, which dated back to the Bronze Age. These were habitations on artificial islands constructed in lakes with stones, wood and earth. Their building must have been a painstaking and very slow process. The primitive dwellings, with their strong fencing and timber stakes, had wet clay hardened to cement them together. This mixed with wattle, covered with mud and dung, dried as hard as rock. Since these houses were surrounded by water, their occupants had to keep fires going. They hung animal skins on the walls. The roofs were thatched with reeds.

There were also ancient burial mounds. None of the country people would touch them or indeed allow anyone to interfere with them. They believed they were the burial plots of the kings and queens of Ireland. It is said vast amounts of treasure money and jewels were buried with them, but it was more than anyone's life was worth to interfere with them.

There were other great houses in my childhood, but I was too young and my memories of them are hazy. Annagh was a holiday home that I learned to love. My first love was that other house, home of my childhood, Saintbury in Killiney, County Dublin. Fantasy, fact, life all interwoven— that's how it was when I was a child. The years rolled by; so many things happened in my life that I did not dwell on those dear days past.

Here to complete my story—I must leap forward in time. I had just left school, and Mother, my brother Jack and I decided to go and visit Annagh. Sadly, poor gentle Uncle Harold had died. He had reverted to Catholicism and Aunt Kate had told him to leave. He died in St Kevin's hostel, Dublin in 1928, and was buried in a pauper's grave. Missing in the man was whatever it takes to survive. Aunt Kate had died suddenly and only Aunt Anna was left. Like Miss Havisham in *Great Expectations*, she lived alone in the crumbling dusty grandeur of the old house, Beatrice her only companion.

It was strange when we arrived to see how everything looked the same: the waterfall by the main gates, the rushing brown water. I could nearly see a little dark-haired girl paddling to look for crayfish under the stones. There was the old ivy-covered house, the tall trees, the rooks cawing— the same scenery, but so many of the actors were gone. An old Beatrice let us in, that big tall woman now shrivelled, her black hair turned white. Only her dark crafty eyes were the same.

Stupidly I said, "Where's Jock?"—the terrier.

"He be gone years ago, Miss. McConnell, too. Took a heart attack, he died. And poor Captain Frazer—a hard woman, Miss Kate. Miss Anna's upstairs. She won't know you. She's in the four-poster bed."

There in the middle of the huge bed was poor old Aunt Anna. She looked at us but did not recognise us. She still wore a tiny Union Jack on top of her head to protect her hair from smoke. When I was a child, I remembered asking her why and she had replied crossly, "Papa and the boys [long ago dead], their smoking discolours my hair."

She was ninety-two. I was glad to see that the visiting health nurse was keeping her clean and tidy. She looked thin and wizened. She was nursing a baby doll, hugging it close and crooning to it. It was an old-fashioned china doll dressed in long clothes. "She won't leave go of that doll for one minute," Beatrice said. "It was their doll—her and Miss Kate's, God rest her, and that dress it's got on was the christening robe they both wore." I looked at the beautiful yellowed lace. Aunt Anna kept rocking the doll and cuddling it up to her.

"She thinks she gave birth to it; she believes it's her baby," said Beatrice. "Who's the father?" Mother said, laughing. "How pathetic, the baby she never had." My brother Jack was the only one who could get through to her. Her faded blue eyes looked at him when he spoke. "How are you, Auntie?" he said in his very British accent. He was then at the Royal Military College, Sandhurst. Aunt Anna told him, "My room revolves, you know. It moves with the sun, rotates so the child and I are always kept warm." Her mind had moved into that strange cocoon of in-betweenness 'twixt life and death.

I could detect the indefinable aura of decay in the room. I noted the acid smell of an old body, lavender water, the damp walls in the room, the yellowed lace of Aunt Anna's nightgown, the torn pink and gold brocade coverlet. To add to the atmosphere, the branch of a fig tree blown by the wind tapped the window-pane every now and then.

The doctor called from Ballinafad. "It won't be long now. I doubt she'll see the morning." Then I understood that another chapter in my life was coming to an end.

My mind went back remembering again. How I had been afraid in the woods that the ghost of poor drowned Aunt Edith would come floating by, her long dark hair still tangled with green weeds. I did not know it then but "little Una," my aunt who had died aged sixteen from tuberculosis, had breathed her last in that big four-poster bed where Aunt Edith's remains had rested, where Aunt Kate had died and where now Aunt Anna was lying.

I stayed to muse—the bed had memories. I remembered that great hank of misery and bitterness, Mrs West, wife of our Saintbury gardener. She was six foot tall and placed in charge of me. She never spoke (or smiled) unless she had to. I recalled the misery of sharing the four-poster bed, of being unable to move all night for fear that she would chastise me. Who or what had cast a woman in a mould like hers, a female who had not a word of kindness for a child. Then there was Nannie, who kept the nursery cupboard locked, hoarding the goodies for her favourites, my two younger sisters. She would not allow me even one chocolate biscuit. I thought of Mother and Aunt Mona, who looked on me in the light of a pet parrot who says "such amusing things." This four-poster bed had seen birth, death, a suicide and had cradled a little child's fear as she had lain there afraid to move, crying silent tears on the head of her teddy bear.

In the cold dark hours of the morning, Grand-aunt Anna died. She was laid out in a fine lawn nightgown and looked so tiny in the big bed. The winds of the previous evening had dropped; the fig tree's branch no longer tapped the window. In my grand-aunt's serene old face one could still see traces of the beautiful girl she once had been. The old house and all its belongings were to be sold. The four-poster bed would probably go in the auction. I wondered if, like bricks and mortar, furniture could retain elements of that which is past and gone. I thought of the wooden cross in the field that stood as a reminder of a beautiful girl who in loneliness and despair had seen fit to take her life. Edith was judged and condemned as unfit to be buried in consecrated ground by Christians who had been told, "Judge not, that ye be not judged."

Two days later Anna Frazer was laid to rest in the family plot at Ardcarne. My brother threw a handful of clay onto the coffin. On a tree nearby a blackbird suddenly burst into song. My eyes filled. I looked across at the vicar.

He smiled and said, "What better requiem."

4

CORODOO

Before letting go of the shadows of the past, I will let my memory return to another stately home, Corodoo, the home of my uncle, Major Edward Frazer. Like Annagh, it was situated near Boyle, in Roscommon, a Tudor-style mansion standing on forty acres. My uncle intended to farm there, but having bought the property, discovered that the land was stony.

As Father remarked, "Eddie was always a damn fool." He did however cover himself in glory in 1914 and was awarded the Croix de Guerre, France's highest award for bravery. He was big and handsome and a great man for the horses and the hunt and known by his fellow huntsmen as the "flying major" for his daring in taking the highest jumps.

One night the major (Uncle Edward to me) got drunk in the officers' mess. His fellow officers made him promise that the following day he would make his way to Hollybrook House, home of the Murphys, a Protestant family. Freda and Beatrice (known as Beattie), the daughters of the house, were "very plain," Freda tall and thin and Beattie small and fat. It was believed that in the unlikely event of matrimony, both would have a substantial dowry! Uncle Eddie was the only one of the four Frazer men to remain true to his Protestant religion. Because he was an officer and a gentleman, he could not go back on his word of honour. He proposed to Miss Freda Murphy and was accepted with great joy. The paradox here is that, despite the fact that the marriage did not begin as a love affair, she bore him a son and a daughter and they lived a long and tranquil life together.

Corodoo, while structurally unlike Saintbury, could have been said to be *en rapport* with it. The interior was decorated with the antelope, buffalo and other big-game heads, shot by my uncles in India; skins of leopard and tiger sprawled on the floor; there were the inevitable regimental pictures, old family portraits and faded sepia photographs of stiffly posed relatives of a bygone age. The furniture was not nearly as nice as at Saintbury. It was mostly heavy Queen Anne and Jacobean and had been inherited from the Murphy family. Nottingham lace curtained the windows, there were aspidistras and there was always dust, but no one seemed to mind it or even to see it.

A slattern known as Maggie helped Aunt Freda and her sister Beattie did the cooking. The major's daughter, Betty, looked after the poultry, the son Ned helped in the running of the small farm which consisted of a few cows, sheep and, of course, horses. The only visitor was the archdeacon who called four times a year. Hence every afternoon the slattern Maggie put on a black-and-white uniform, in case, as the mistress said, "the archdeacon might call."

Betty Frazer told me the following anecdote. She did not seem to think it funny but *I* did. The archdeacon had given notice of his arrival. Protocol was thus: Maggie was to be dressed in uniform, Irish stew would be served on the best dinner service. Georgian silver candlesticks might adorn the long oak dining-room table but the silver was unpolished and the Waterford glass a bit dusty. (The master and mistress did not notice such details, but kept to correct procedures like passing the port to the left, the wine to the right.) When after dessert, the major announced, "You may smoke," this was the signal for the ladies to retire. All this was duly rehearsed.

Then the servant Maggie disappeared and the mistress was quite distraught. What if the archdeacon called? By the second day the gardaí were alerted. Ned, the major's son, was hopping with excitement. He loved reading murder mysteries and kept repeating gleefully, "Maggie's been done in." Everyone thought it a dreadful thing to say but the ten-year-old boy had planted the seed of doubt.

It was Betty's job to bring in the cows for milking. She had to cross a little bridge to the fields. It had rained heavily for days and the ditch was full of water. As she crossed the bridge, she noticed bulging above the waterline below a large plastic bag. Betty paled. She felt faint with fear. She found a long stick and poked; there was something fleshy and pliable in the bag. Her screams were terrible as she raced home, the rain beating down on her. Aunt Freda and her sister Beattie were in a bad state of nerves, worsened by Betty's news. Uncle Edward automatically assumed a military stance. "Everyone must fall in and I shall head the search-party," he announced. They sallied forth—the major, clad in oilskins and wellington boots, followed by Shannon, the yard man, with a shotgun, Betty snivelling, carrying a length of rope, Ned with a wheelbarrow with a large wooden box at the ready. The sisters, Freda and Beattie, clutched each other under a large umbrella. Across the sodden fields they marched, the rain coming down in stair-rods. They reached the bridge. The major, who knew all the correct manoeuvres, roared instructions to Shannon. With the aid of a rope and a rake, they heaved the large bulging wet sack onto the bank.

Shannon said, "The ladies would be as well not looking." His face was dead white. He removed his cap and with reverence blessed himself.

The major, who was a bigoted Protestant, barked, "Cut out the popery and get on with it."

Shannon slit the sack with his knife. A horn appeared. He crossed himself again. "Holy Mother, it's auld Nick himself."

"You damned fool!" barked the major. "It's a bloody cow."

Back to the house they trailed, the rain pelting down. Standing in the portico was Maggie, a battered suitcase beside her. She had, she explained, gone to visit her family in Ballinafad. The storm was that bad, they had kept her overnight.

"Damned fool of a woman should have told us," said the major, "but then she never was fully *compos mentis*."

"What's that?" asked Ned.

"Not the full shilling."

"Get off now, my girl, and change into your uniform. The archdeacon might call," said the mistress.

Back into the dusty old house they trudged: the irate major, his plain wife, fat old Aunt Beattie, Betty snivelling, a disappointed son, Ned. Maggie went off to change into her uniform and Shannon mumbled his way back to his yard.

5

SHANGRI-LA

Before I let go of these anecdotes from the past, I would like to say a little about my grandmother Frazer. My father always referred to her as "that damned old woman." She was patronising to him because his father, though knighted by Queen Victoria, had made his money in "trade"—he was head of a firm which made feather beds. She would say mockingly, "Charles, poor Charles, he is very small." My father was about 5ft 10, but the Frazer men were at least four inches taller.

Mother used to take me as a small child to visit Grandmother in Shangri-La, her home in Sorrento Terrace, Dalkey. Aunt Mona lived with her, although Grandmother used to say, "Mona lives *off* me." It was a three-storey house with a basement, and the back faced the sea, giving a beautiful view of Dalkey Sound. There were steps at the bottom of the garden where you could climb with care down to a bit of pebbly beach. When the sea came in, it covered the beach. If you could swim or owned a boat, it was perfect.

Grandmother and Aunt Mona were very rich. Mother

said that they lived off capital. I did not know what this meant. They were always asking, "Was there a dividend from China?" Their money came from the Hong Kong and Shanghai Bank. Before the Boxer Rebellion in 1900 they had lived in Tientsin, where my grandfather was a doctor.

Mother used get desperate if the dividends did not turn up. She said she was fed up "trying novenas" and one night announced that she would sell her soul to the devil for a dividend. (I was terrified.) She said: "Here I am, Satan, in return for a dividend." She said the devil was much quicker with requests. I really think even she got a fright when two days later the long envelope with Chinese stamps arrived. It was the dividend. Mother said she never invoked the devil again.

Aunt Mona had plenty of furs, clothes and diamonds. Grandmother had beautiful rings, one on every finger. They had had a special safe made in which to keep their jewellery. It was under a rug on the drawing-room floor. There was a small ring and if you pulled it a box came up. No one ever discovered it. Aunt Mona had a collie dog called Roy. He was never taken for a walk and grew so fat that no one could tell what breed he was.

I never liked my grandmother, yet she adored me. I was the *enfant terrible*. I used sing, dance and recite for her. Since she had lived most of her life in China, the house was full of beautiful Chinese furniture, wall-hangings, ornaments and pictures. One object I loved was the prayer wheel: a round box on the end of an ivory stick. You could open the box and put in one written prayer, as the Chinese did. There were beaded weights on the box so as you swung

it, it turned. The Chinese believed that with every turn of
the wheel the prayer was said, and they would sit meditating
and swinging the prayer wheel round and round.

Grandmother wore her hair in a top knot. Her house
dresses had high Prussian collars to cover her ageing neck.
Her clothes tended to be a mixture of Samo-Foo (loose
blouson tops) and trousers so baggy that they looked like
a long skirt. European clothes were worn for going out. She
spoke Chinese in two dialects: Cantonese and the one used
in Hong Kong. It must be admitted she was a very clever
woman, a brilliant pianist, bilingual in French and Italian,
a skilled player of bridge and also of mah-jong, that difficult
Chinese game. Mother said it was vulgar because the game,
usually played by four people, involved the four winds and
hence players had to say "Pass your wind" to each other.
Grandmother said, "It's your mother who is vulgar, finding
double meanings in mah-jong!" Mah-jong is Chinese for
sparrow, "bird of a thousand songs," they say, because it
doesn't sing. Chinese humour is different from ours, as is
their way of thinking.

Grandmother owned a villa in Monte Carlo and she
and Aunt Mona went there every year in the early nineteen
twenties. They avoided the hot sun, like all the ladies of
their time, but haunted the casino, where Grandmother
lost a small fortune. Aunt Mona travelled with her as a
companion-help. Grandmother referred to her as a "hanger-
on" and used audibly to sigh, "What else could a spinster
do?" In fact they were both compulsive gamblers.

Poor Aunt Mona once met a man called Percy
McDermott, who was related to the McDermott Roe, Prince

of Coolavin, an old Irish title. Marriage was on the cards but Grandmother was having none of it; she needed her companion-help so she feigned illness, and Aunt Mona, who (like all the girls) adored her mother, left her lover and stayed with her until she died.

Grandmother had once been beautiful, tall and dark, with strange nearly black eyes. She was born Eva Kennet in England and brought up Catholic but lapsed and began to dabble in spiritualism. She claimed to have a string of ancestors going back to the Plantagenet kings. At the age of eighteen she met and married Dr John Lovatt Frazer, a man of Scottish birth. She said she hated sex though she bore him four sons and four daughters. She and her husband separated and took it in turns to stay with the children at their home Riversdale in County Roscommon. Grandfather would stay a year and then Grandmother arrived for her year of duty. Duty it was because she loved none of them, with the exception of one son who was killed at the first battle of the Somme in 1916. John Frazer was brave, dashing and debonair and she never got over his death. He had run (under gunfire) to pick up my father, who had been shot in the shoulder, and in so doing was shot in the head.

I was only five when Grandmother died in Shangri-La. The year was 1925. Mother took me to see her when she was dying. I had never seen anyone dying before and I was very frightened. A nurse (she had two) was padding about the darkened room; Grandmother had a mask over her face and her breathing was a rasping noise. I ran out of the room. The funeral service was private and held in the Protestant church, St Patrick's, in Dalkey. After that the remains were taken all the way back to Boyle, County Roscommon and hence to Ardcarne, the Frazer burial plot.

One day a man in a van with ISPCA on its side came to take poor Roy away, and he barked and barked. I knew he did not want to go. Upset, I asked Aunt Mona where the dog was going. She said, "Auntie has to sell the house and Roy would have no home or a garden to play in."

"But where is the man taking Roy?"

Mother intervened. "The man is going to arrange for him to go to the dogs' heaven."

They were all telling me lies, I knew. Roy was looking out of the van. He had such sad eyes, amber like the tiger in the bay window. That was the saddest animal of all— made into a rug with the head intact. Grandmother told me, "There is an old Chinese proverb: amber is the heart of the tiger turned to stone." I said to her, "My eyes are blue; will blue be the heart of a child turned to stone?"

"You are a strange little child, I hope your heart never turns to stone." I did not understand. I did not cry for Grandmother. I cried only for that poor dog.

6

SAILING AND JIMMY MOONEY

I met Jimmy Mooney on a blind date. I was twenty-six. Mother kept saying, "It's time you got a move on and got married." We were at the same party and he saw me home. I did not even like him for at least six months. He was very quiet and shy but when he was on his own stamping ground, the Royal St George Yacht Club in Dun Laoghaire and among his friends, he went into reverse; he was a terrible tease to the point of reducing some of the girls to tears, and, of course, talked about his great passion, sailing, until I nearly went berserk! I had no interest. Jimmy was a dentist and worked with his father, Billy Mooney, in their Fitzwilliam Street practice. Obviously clever, he qualified in dentistry when too young to practise, so he did medicine in the interval and became a doctor as well.

Our courtship was for me very unhappy in one aspect. My father openly disapproved because we came from totally different backgrounds. He was Protestant and I was Roman Catholic, a notably different ethos; so, of course, I could not bring him home to our beautiful house, Saintbury, in Killiney. On the occasion of our engagement dinner party

Jimmy, his father and stepmother, were put at the end of the long dining-room table, as far away from my father as possible. He all but ignored them; the only conversation exchanged was after dinner. On entering the large drawing-room, Billy Mooney went over to Father, determined to be friendly and engage in normal chat. He said, "That's a beautiful view of Killiney Bay." My father looked at him over his pince-nez glasses and said, "Yes, it is a fine view and the weather is mild for the time of the year." And those were the only words my father ever spoke to Jimmy's father. In spite of Father's terrible opposition, we married in 1948.

The Mooney family: father, mother, Jimmy and brother Bob, lived in Howth. Jimmy's sailing career started there in an International 12 dinghy when he was about four. His father, had given him and his brother a dinghy each. Jimmy's first taste of sailing had been at the age of six months when the family were in an overnight race from Dun Laoghaire to the Isle of Man. Jimmy had been carried in a hammock in the forecastle.

As Jimmy got older, he began to take part in offshore races with his father. He continued to sail the 12 at Howth until his father bought the *Mermaid Minx* which they kept at Dun Laoghaire. They had great success and won many races. The Mooneys moved from Howth to Monkstown in 1942. Jimmy then bought a Wag Bluebird and continued to sail with average success during the Emergency. In 1945 after the war a number of dinghy sailors felt there should be a national body to control the International 12 dinghy class in Ireland. These people, who came from all parts of

Ireland, had been racing since 1923. Jimmy was the prime mover in this venture. Already in 1943 he had founded the Irish Dinghy Racing Association. He became interested in dinghy design and helped produce a new fourteen-foot dinghy. Many boats were built during 1944 to the design that Jimmy had helped shape.

In 1946 the body known as the Irish Yachting Association was set up to further Irish participation in international events. Jimmy had played a large part in its conception. Thanks to him and his fellow enthusiasts, Ireland was able to send a yachting team to the 1948 Olympics in England. In 1947 he organised the first Dinghy Week to be held in Dun Laoghaire and the first Helmsman's Championship of Ireland for Fireflies, these small craft having become popular.

I was not told this story about one of them until nineteen years after Jimmy's death. Shortly after the arrival of the first Fireflies in March 1947, Jimmy decided to take his new boat for a sail single-handed. It was blowing hard and the seas were rough. While battling the high waves, the little boat suddenly overturned, and there were no boats near to rescue him. The Mooneys' house was not far from the sea and it was by sheer chance that his father saw the incident. Billy had a powerful telescope, but whatever (or whoever) made him decide to look out to sea on a day when the yachting season had not begun, we shall never know. Billy loaded a small rowing dinghy on to a trolley and dashed to the slip at Seapoint. He launched it, rowed manfully and with much difficulty through the high seas and rescued his son. What a very strange thing fate is!

In 1948 Jimmy won the Olympic Firefly trials. In 1949 he organised the first Irish international team to sail against England. In 1952 he was chosen as reserve in the Finn Class Olympic yachting team, for the Olympics in Helsinki. In 1953 he joined the bigger yacht class, the Dragons, and won the Duke of Edinburgh's cup at Cultra, on Belfast Lough. Happily I was there to join the celebrations with him. Lord Wakehurst (then Governor General of Northern Ireland) and Lady Wakehurst were in residence then, and she, representing the Queen, presented Jimmy with the Edinburgh Cup. The funniest part of it was that the phone rang at home later that day and I answered it. A frightfully laid back voice said, "This is a priority call from Buckingham Palace." I thought it was my son Billy, messing, and said, "Oh yeah, stuff yourself." It rang again and a rather irate gentleman announced, "I am the Duke of Edinburgh's secretary and I am to read you a telegram." It read: "Well done, Jimmy. Heartiest congratulations, Philip." The confirmation arrived later.

Jimmy won the Edinburgh Cup in 1958. I did not like having it in the house because I was worried that it might be stolen. Our small three-up three-down house in Dundela Park, Glenageary, was not the proper setting. In 1953, Jimmy started a Dublin Bay Sailing Club for juniors; lessons were given free by the best yachtsmen. One year Ireland sent crews to Naples in the Dragon class, sailed by Jimmy Mooney. He was part of a crew that secured three Olympic bronze medals for Ireland in sailing in London in 1948, Helsinki in 1952 and Rome in 1960. Nineteen sixty was another Olympic year and Irish dinghy racing was short one hand to send a team to compete. Jimmy got a brainwave. Why not a boat show instead? The idea was immediately gunned down by his fellow yachtsmen but Jimmy was a fighter. He finally got CIE to agree to provide Busaras, Dublin's central bus station, as a venue free. That very first Irish Boat Show proved to be a brilliant success. In the midsixties Jimmy founded and edited a sailing magazine, *Irish Yachting*, which was initially sponsored by a committee of sailing people. Then in 1970 he started the Dun Laoghaire sailing school which in different hands is still going.

While he had a great sense of humour and was a terrible tease, Jimmy was a perfectionist, a hard taskmaster who did not suffer fools. He never asked anyone to do something he would not do himself. In one particular race in the Dragon, he had been unusually severe on his two-man crew. Dublin Bay races always finished by rounding a mark off the Coal Harbour and, if the wind was westerly, running easily down the fairway to the finishing line off St Michael's wharf. On this occasion after rounding the Coal Harbour mark, it was a straight downwind leg to the finish. As Jimmy's boat neared the line, the crew fixed the main boom and spinnaker in position and when the boat crossed, the two chaps shook hands, dived overboard and swam ashore, leaving Jimmy to sort out the shambles. They were picked up out of the water by Billy Mooney in his boat. Everyone said Jimmy got the message and his mutinous crew remained friendly.

I never went out sailing. I have always been afraid of the sea, so much so that my fear almost amounts to a phobia. I went out in all weathers during our courtship, and Jimmy thought it amusing to take me out when there was a heavy swell, or even to sail into the mail-boat's wash. The waves looked mountainous from our small boat and I was petrified. After our marriage, though, that was it! I went sailing once in our twenty-three years. Jimmy always said it made for a better relationship that I did not sail since marital sailing sometimes caused fierce arguments. I was proud of my husband's nautical abilities but I always felt apprehensive about his health. Funnily enough, he was always apprehensive about mine.

7

YOUNG MARRIEDS

My father died in 1952. He never forgave me for marrying in a Protestant church and duly cut me out of his will. Mother survived him by thirteen years. I had no idea when I married that I was taking on a "job"—the hardest I had ever done. Jimmy's mother had economised, scrimped and saved, baked, cooked, and mended shirt collars and cuffs when they frayed. She used turn out one room completely every day and polished everything so there was no dust in the house. But I could not match this. Cleanliness, threadbare carpets, hand-sewn religious samplers—"Christ is the unseen guest in this house"—no alcohol or smoking; then the plus side, home-made bread and cakes, and truth and honesty abounding—it was a different ethos. There was no contact between Protestants and Roman Catholics in the nineteen fifties in Ireland and one set did not know how the other lived.

When I first married I could not cook. Mother used send Pat, the cook from Saintbury, down to me twice a week. He cooked and stacked up the fridge with lots of "readies" and for a short time I fooled Jimmy into thinking the culinary efforts were mine. The new life became a nightmare. I was an unpaid cook-housekeeper and I hated it! However, Pauline, my first baby, brought me great joy, especially since I had been so ill during the pregnancy that my doctor doubted that the baby would survive. This made her doubly precious.

We had very little money and the house had to be furnished. Jimmy decided that we would go to a cheap shop on the quays along the Liffey and there we bought poor quality furniture, little better than varnished plywood. Jimmy said we would gradually replace it with good stuff. We never did. I had grown up appreciating beautiful things and I simply detested the junk. Our son, William Raymond, was born two-and-a-half years after Pauline. "That's it," Jimmy said, "we have our family: a girl and a boy!" I couldn't agree; I wanted four, even six, babies.

Mother visited our little house frequently. She had a way of becoming a child with children and they loved her, even though she would say, "I would rather spend a day in jail breaking stones than mind them." Aunt Mona was our usual babysitter and she had unending patience. Jimmy, who was never superstitious, believed that Aunt Mona was responsible for strange, perhaps supernatural, incidents in our most unghostly little house. There was knocking on the doors at night and sudden gusts of cold air. Mother and Aunt Mona said they sensed something in the house that should not be there. When I told Jimmy, he laughed but then he put on his "I-wonder" expression. Late one summer's evening I heard him messing about in the attic. I ran upstairs and called, "What are you doing up there?"

"Bringing it down."

"Bringing what down?"

He emerged from the attic with cobwebs in his hair, and stepped carefully down the ladder with a very long narrow box. He kept laughing. I said, "Don't open it. I don't want to see it."

"It's only a musical instrument." He put the box on the ground. "Now Aunt Mona and your mother will be interested." He opened the box. In it was a human skeleton with all parts intact. Jimmy told me he had bought it when he was doing medicine. It had once been a man. I said, "Get him out! That's terrible—a remains in our attic. If he was once a human being, you have to get a proper burial for him." Jimmy kept on laughing. I did my first job of laying out, I folded the hands and said a silent prayer for a soul departed long long ago. That night I saw Jimmy putting the box in the boot of the car. I'm pretty certain it was dumped in the sea!

Jimmy and his father decided that dentistry was more lucrative than medicine. Besides, there were six tenants in the large Georgian house, which one day Jimmy would inherit. His only brother, Bob, who was a surgeon-captain in the Royal Navy, would inherit Billy's home, Ardfern, a lovely house facing the sea on the corner of Bullock Harbour in Dalkey. Before our marriage, Jimmy and Billy lived together in the Monkstown house. Billy had said to me, "If you marry Jimmy, I'll settle for that 'old one' that's always after me!" He must have fancied her, even though he used to say, "I can't go into the National Yacht Club; she's always propped up at the bar." Her name was Mildred

Douglas and she used sit over her gin-and-tonic waiting for the lads to come in from racing. She was fifty-six, very plump, with pretty auburn (tinted!) hair, dimples and a fixed smile. Even when she was in bad humour, the smile stayed, as if printed on. She reminded me, not surprisingly, of the Cheshire cat in *Alice's Adventures in Wonderland* who would disappear, leaving only the smile behind.

After six months of pursuing him she got him! Unlike Billy's first wife, she was not holy and the religious items disappeared. Drink was kept in the house and she smoked. She did not economise but spent his money—and he seemed very happy!

Jimmy was a man of his time, a good provider—my house-keeping money (however little) was always on the table for me every Saturday morning. School fees and all bills were paid and he saw to it that I got a good holiday every year. Apart from that, he would bring me unexpected presents of boxes of chocolates and flowers. All the time I missed Saintbury so much. Sometimes if I could get someone to mind the children, I would take the Killiney bus and go and sit (hidden) in the garden. I would look longingly at the house but I was afraid to go in in case my father was at home. After his death, Mother moved to a lovely apartment overlooking the sea in Monkstown. Aunt Mona went too, as ever "hanging on." The apartment was quite like Saintbury, especially the drawing-room.

After Pauline's birth, Mother was always on at me: "Why aren't you expecting?" She loved babies, not so much the children they grew into. The rearing of children in love and care has always seemed to me vitally important. One of the things that still makes me angry is the presumption of the religious orders of my own childhood in thinking that they knew how to educate children in their schools. In one of my boarding-schools talking at meals was not permitted. A nun on a rostrum would read from St Thomas Aquinas or the letters of St Augustine. Consequently when I came home, I sat at the table like a dumbo, with not a word to say. The sisters stifled and frightened us with the stern Almighty, the Devil and the need for penance. I have never forgiven them.

On my mother's visiting days, my children would watch from the upstairs windows. Often they would cry delightedly, "She's gone into the wrong house again!" In fairness, our little suburban house looked much the same as the other houses in the street, though of course the garden and decor were different. Mother invariably missed the house. In those days we did not bother to lock our back doors, and one day she had marched into number forty-five (we lived at number sixty-two), looked round the hall and had shouted up the stairs, "What in the world did you re-do the place for? It was much nicer before; it's a horrible colour now." An irate lady came down the stairs and said, "I think you're in the wrong house."

A special treat for Pauline and Billy (they were very young then) was that Grandma would take them for short walks. One of the children invariably suggested, "Grannie, let's have a bonfire." So with whatever bits of paper and cigarette packets she could find in her handbag she would make a little pile and put a match to them. One day, down a laneway at the back of our road, Grannie made her bonfire as usual. It was a dry summer and suddenly the small blaze became a serious fire. An irate man came charging down his garden shouting, "You bloody maniac, you have set the place on fire." Mother said, "How dare you! The children and I saw the fire and we are trying to put it out." The man was full of apologies and invited them in to tea!

I became pregnant again when Billy was about three and, though I was awfully sick from the start, I was delighted. Jimmy on the other hand was not. I decided to keep the news to myself for as long as possible. Mother's eagle eye annoyed me and Aunt Mona was always watching. The sickness passed. I felt well again and by the sixteenth week there had been no comment from anyone. One evening we decided to go to the pictures and since Aunt Mona had flu our "daily" came to babysit. We were going to see *Ben Hur*. At five o'clock I had cramps in my tummy and Jimmy gave me an Alka-Seltzer saying it must be the lobster from the day before. I felt terribly tired and nauseous and did not want to go out. "It will do you good to go," insisted Jimmy. On the drive into town I felt better and once in the cinema began to enjoy the film. Suddenly, I was gripped in a vice-like pain. I whispered to Jimmy, "I have to get to the Ladies quick." The woman in charge in the powder room looked at me anxiously as I bolted into a loo. The pain got worse and I discovered that I was haemorrhaging. I called out to the attendant, "Get my husband, Dr Mooney, third row from the front circle right side." That woman was wonderful; she got me out and had me lying down covered with towels when Jimmy arrived. Very quickly ambulance men were there. Then hospital, lights, an injection for the pain. Someone said, "That's it; now push." I looked. The tiny baby was lying in blood, curled up dead. A nurse whispered, "We baptised him." My little son went into eternity with some recognition and dignity.

Years later, a nice priest said to me, "Why not name him right now?" We called him Simon and this little poem is his epitaph:

> Born out of my body and my blood,
> Why did you leave me so soon to wing
> Your way back into eternity?
> Why did I conceive you, little one,
> To know the agony of losing you?
> What could I have ever done
> To lie here helpless, hear you whimper,
> Watch you die, my baby son?

The miscarriage happened on a Saturday, so I was at home in time for Mother's Thursday visit. She never knew what had happened. She would have been terribly upset, having lost a little boy herself at six months. This was different, but every grief and every pain must indeed be different.

8

DOGS AND ASHES

Christmases were different after our marriage, though I always put up a special Christmas lunch for Mother and Aunt Mona, making sure that everything was very nice and proper. Mother was very particular about the niceties and I was relieved when she said she was well pleased with my efforts.

She always gave us all the same presents every year. This was especially nice for Jimmy, because, apart from bottles of whiskey and gin, she gave him six Waterford glasses—tumblers, sherry glasses, liqueur glasses—so that he built up a lovely collection. I was given a Brown Thomas gift token. Pauline always got the same doll and the same clothes for it. Billy was invariably given a conjuring set, and Wendy, eight years younger than Pauline and six years younger than Billy, the same fluffy white teddy bear. These were all done up in rough brown paper and hairy string. At the end of the festivities, a friend would bring Mother and Aunt Mona home. With one on each arm he used guide them to the car and, on arrival at their home, this kindly man escorted each lady to her bedroom and placed her on her bed. Hats on, coats, handbags over their arms, they slept the sleep of total joy oblivious—until the next day!

Billy and Mildred Mooney had a lovely house which they called Ardfern. It was situated in Sandycove and had a garden sloping down to the sea. Their Christmas dinner was always served in the evening, not all that long after my Christmas lunch, so none of us had any appetite. It was a great family occasion. The grown-ups sat round a well-appointed large round table and the grandchildren, eight in number at this time, were accommodated at two smaller ones. Mildred's two sons had married two Pats and Billy's two sons had married two Sheilas, so there were big Pat and little Pat and big Sheila and little Sheila in the Yuletide company. Silver, lace, candlelight and vintage wine brought back something of the grace of days gone by— that is until Bridie, the help, handed round the potatoes in the pot they were cooked in and Mildred greedily ate that part of the turkey known as "the pope's nose."

The grandest guest was always Jimmy's brother Bob, the surgeon-captain, who came with his wife and their three children. Mildred and Billy were two old snobs and treated Bob and his family like royalty. The rest of us were very much second-class citizens! After dinner came the family entertainment. Billy played his tin whistle and he was really good. On one occasion he announced he had a special surprise guest for us. We waited with bated breath. Up went the lights and in flew a figure in old-fashioned long johns with a placard pinned to his back. It had the words Ronnie Delaney printed on it. Round and round the room he ran, knees high, amid peals of laughter. Less gripping was a recitation by Arthur Page, a cousin of Billy's. He was a rather solemn man and always recited a monologue called "A Banker Transferred." It will be no surprise to hear that he was a retired bank official. We were always too bored to listen. All I remember was that every verse ended with the words, "a banker transferred."

Once Mildred's son, Don Douglas, mentioned my niece, Mia Farrow, a great girl who has seven adopted children, plus four of her own. His mother, she of the fixed smile, Mrs Billy Mooney the second (known behind her back as just Mildred or Grannie Mooney), and still with the smile intact, announced, "We do not talk of people like that in this house." She knew I could not do or say anything. It was Christmas, the season of peace and goodwill.

The very best entertainment I can recall was given by my Wendy and Gordon Douglas. (Mildred's grandson), both then about six. They put on a puppet show and everything was great until the language of the puppets became very rude and Mildred stopped the show. One Christmas when my son Billy was about fifteen he told a silent room how he would like a sex change. He had been reading about a man who became the famous model girl Tula. He had us in stitches.

Life went on in suburbia and I enjoyed every day of it with my growing children. Jimmy continued to practise dentistry but he had now become the big star of the sailing world. The word yuppie was unheard of in the nineteen forties and fifties but the elite of the sailing world were definitely of that calibre: money no object, wonderful fibreglass yachts, round-the-world races, fast cars as big as tanks, overdressed wives, sons in public schools.

The style at the dances was phenomenal. Clothes were much cheaper then, and Maureen, my actress sister, used to send home great boxes of clothes known in the family as "charity parcels." Mother would send the word, "There's a charity parcel from America," and my sisters and I would fall upon the contents greedily—poor Mother hardly got anything. She always hid the best things for me. I was even in matters like this her favourite. She loved me and my brother Jack and did not, though she said she tried, love her other three daughters. The American boxes were far from charity. They contained lovely, hardly worn dresses, suits, beautiful hats and handbags, glamorous dance-frocks. Once Maureen sent us two glittering evening-jackets, one in silver sequins and one in gold. Hollywood was full of glamour in the forties and fifties, and women's clothes were feminine; there were no blue jeans and runners. So I was well able to compete with the glitterati at the yacht-club functions.

Mother was very good at telling fortunes with the cards and reading palms. Actually she was psychic, as am I. She would never cut the cards for me or read my hand, not for a thousand pounds. Now with hindsight I know why. However, one particular day she was fiddling about with the cards and she said, "His soul is yet to be born." I asked "Whose soul?" and she said, "Jimmy's. He's in for some illness, but he won't die yet." Then she said, "Put the cards away. One shouldn't play around with them." Yet she was always playing around with them herself.

We kept budgies in a large cage in our sun-porch extension. I was cleaning out the cage one day when one of the birds flew into my face and, before I could catch her, she had flown out of the open hall window. The sky was black and heavy drops of rain began to fall. The brilliant little bluebird, Heidi, delighted in her moment of freedom. I was frantic. I knew the magpies would get her; they could hardly miss the prettiest of the birds. I called to no avail and suddenly she flew up and away. Mother said, "When the bluebird flies away, happiness flies out the window." In China, the bluebird symbolises happiness. Sad to say, the first dark clouds were dimming the horizon.

Jimmy became ill and I knew it had to be serious when he was prepared to miss work. He said to me, "Ring up my secretary and tell her to cancel today's appointments. I'll be in tomorrow." He wasn't. The doctor confirmed that he had mumps. Jimmy was always a dreadful patient; even with a cold, he was at death's door. I dreaded the prospect but the poor chap got really ill and developed orchitis. I always think the name is like some rare tropical flower but it causes pain and swelling in the testicles and can lead to impotence. Of course every father on the road wanted to come and visit Jimmy. In those days we had neither pill nor condoms. Sadly Jimmy's illness was not to end there; he got jaundice and meningitis. We were told he would have to be moved out to the fever hospital, which was a long way away at Cherry Orchard. The ambulance arrived and poor Jimmy was carried off. The children and I all cried as he was driven away. Billy Mooney and Mildred drove us out twice a week to visit him, but we could look at him only through glass since stringent precautions had to be observed. In due course Jimmy came home, but I always felt that my husband was never quite the same again. After the three weeks' hospitalisation he looked very frail.

Jimmy was a keen angler and an equally keen fisherman. He always tied his own flies. I found it fascinating to watch him tickling trout and then picking them out of the water hypnotised! I have seen him hypnotise mice, dogs and cats. I always swore too that he hypnotised me in the dental chair and I used to say, "That was the reason I married you." The story of the mouse was weird. It ran out of the kitchen through the hall and darted into the living-room. I jumped up on a chair like a woman in a cartoon. It's just that I hate the way they run so quickly. This little mouse ran up the long curtains in the living-room. Jimmy said, "Watch." He went over very quietly and stared and stared at the mouse. The next thing he had it in his hand, immobile! He opened the french windows and put it on the ground. It still did not move until he gave it a tap and off it ran. Jimmy had beautiful eyes, a strange hazel green, and though he treated his hypnotic powers as a joke, I think they went much deeper than he was aware of.

Whatever activities Jimmy pursued during the week, he kept Sundays for the family. We usually lunched at the Bel Air Hotel in Ashford, County Wicklow and afterwards the children played in the beautiful grounds. We always had a dog but it really belonged to Jimmy. Every dog we got was to be trained as his gundog. He said I spoiled them all and turned them into lap-dogs. Our first dog, Johnnie, an elegant golden cocker, bolted at the first gunshot, so he became my pet. Sadly, one day as he was carrying his weekly bone across the road, he was run over. I was very upset. The second, Gypsy, a black-and-white setter with a touch of collie, ran off with the precious pheasant and ate it. He was a wild creature, not too trustworthy, but he loved his family. He was put down aged sixteen-and-a-half. The sweetest of all was Tony, a golden labrador. He charged after the shot game, but only when he felt like it. He got round Jimmy by bringing his slippers to him every night. He developed nephritis, a kidney disease which in dogs is terminal. He was nine years when he died. I have never been without a dog. What is it that makes some of us love pets while others are just indifferent?

When I was a very small child in Saintbury we had a fat black cocker spaniel also called Tony. When he died, he was immediately replaced by an identical dog. Mother's idea was to have a Tony in perpetuity. When I saw the second one I remember saying, "He looks younger!" Mother said, "He's been on a tonic; that's why!" One day when I was about fifteen and home from boarding-school, I asked, "Where's Tony?" Mother said, "Here he is," and a younger slimmer black cocker bounded in. I burst out laughing and said, "Oh, for heaven's sake, you can't expect me to go on believing you."

But perhaps Mother was right. The dog *per se* is not of prime importance. It's the dog spirit we respond to. But then I can believe what I like; it's about the only freedom we still retain.

One day Jimmy had to tell me that Miss Flossie Johns,

a dear little old lady I had once met, had died in Devon. She had been a lifelong friend of Dolly, his late mother. Flossie used visit Ireland every year. We knew she loved the country but we were amazed to hear that in her will she had asked that her ashes be scattered by Billy and Jimmy on Killiney Hill. Jimmy was a great DIY man and our garage was fitted out with Black-and-Decker equipment and other tools. Everything was immaculate, as in his dental surgery. I do not know why I went into the garage about nine o'clock one warm June evening. There on the work bench was a large wooden box addressed to Dr A J Mooney from a firm of undertakers and embalmers in Devon.

I felt a goose walk over my grave and rushed indoors. My spouse had his feet on the mantelpiece, his regular pose because of varicose veins, and his head in *The Irish Times*. "Jimmy," I said, "this place is getting like a horror movie: first a skeleton in the attic and now cremated ashes in the garage!" He was unperturbed. "The father will be up at ten o'clock and we'll go up Killiney Hill for the scatterin'." I got him to go to the garage with me. He split open the box with a wrench. Inside was a large plastic casket with a cross on the lid. "That's her," Jimmy said. I felt awful. In Ireland one is so conscious of the tremendous respect shown to the dead. Anyway, father and son soon drove off with the small casket, and their two dogs, a labrador and a pointer. Later, Jimmy told me what happened.

The two dogs ran ahead of them as they climbed the hill in the summer twilight; Billy had the casket tucked under his arm. When they reached the top, where the Victoria monument points heavenwards, they paused to look out towards Dublin where the city lights were already starting to twinkle. Then they turned to view that beautiful uncluttered coastline, Ireland's Bay of Naples, the long sweep of beach and beyond the purple Wicklow mountains. This was where a little English lady, as delicate as Dresden china, wished all that remained of her mortality to be scattered. Billy opened the casket and, facing towards the sea and coastline, said, "This is the best spot, Jimmy."

There were more ashes in the casket than he had bargained for. Billy tried to throw them outward. As if from nowhere, a sudden off-sea breeze blew up and the ashes blew back into their faces! Hair and clothes were covered. Even the dogs got a sprinkling. Jimmy said it was quite macabre. Killiney Hill had once been a centre of druid worship. Maybe the spirits of the druids were showing their dislike of this ceremony. When Jimmy came home he was still laughing and continued to splutter as he brushed the ashes off the labrador. I said to him, "You don't get into bed beside me unless you have a bath and wash your hair. The whole thing is creepy." That night I dreamed of a white bird flying out over the sea at Killiney Bay. I felt better. Poor little lady.

9

BIRTH, DEATH AND ACCIDENTS

In 1957, I became pregnant again. Jimmy's mumps had not made any difference. I was delighted and so was Mother. Jimmy was not; he had decided on two children. "Pity about you; there's going to be three," I said.

Years before when I had been at boarding-school at the Convent of the Assumption in West Kensington, I used to gaze from the window of my little room down at the statue of Peter Pan in Kensington Gardens. I had always loved JM Barrie's story. Then I used day-dream how one day I would have a son called Peter and a daughter called Wendy. But Jimmy took over the names. He announced Pauline Anne for our daughter and William Raymond for our son. Then I lost a baby boy because of my miscarriage at sixteen weeks; but I had named him Simon (called Peter), so I was determined that if I had a girl she would be Wendy. It was a happy pregnancy and a quick birth. She was baptised Gwendoline Marie, because there was no Wendy listed in the Book of Saints, but she will always be Wendy. Mother was not pleased. "You must be disappointed that it's not a boy," she said. In fact no one was disappointed. We were all delighted, and Pauline, now aged eight, took over some of the mothering of the new baby.

Jimmy phoned me one morning at ten o'clock.

"Yes," I said apprehensively.

"I'm afraid it's your mother." I knew she had gone.

"Is she dead?" I asked. "I'm afraid she is." "Do you want me to come home?"

"No, I don't want you to come home."

It was 25 July 1963.

Mother had died in her sleep. There are no words to describe how I felt—still feel. Come hell or high water, and there was plenty of both, she and I were a team. A strange kind of loving, but love it was. The little bluebird's flight indeed had begun to bring ill luck. One day Jimmy arrived in for his evening meal looking tense. "Mildred has cancer; it's terminal." She had been for an X-ray and, knowing she was a smoker, the doctor took in her lungs. He had given her only a few months to live. The following day while I was shopping I had a bad fall. Jimmy came home to find me badly bruised and concussed. The doctor came and insisted on my spending a few days in bed. "More bad luck; is it ever going to stop?" Jimmy said.

Yet Mildred was adamant that we take the motoring holiday that we had been planning. I could see that she was dying. Her daughter-in-law, Pat, said that she could not shampoo her head because of all the secondary tumours that had appeared on it. Before leaving we called up to say goodbye to her. She was trying to be very chirpy. I said, "We'll come and see you when we get back."

"Indeed you won't. I'll be up to see you," she bravely retorted.

Jimmy of course drove. Poor Billy was given the job of navigator and so he sat with road-maps in hand the whole time. The beginning was fine. We started out dressed in our new clothes. I had bought a turquoise blue coat that I later came to curse because it was too warm. The initial route was Dublin and then by road and ferry to London. We had two pleasant days showing the children the Changing of the Guard, Madame Tussaud's and the pigeons in Trafalgar Square. Then on to Dover where we boarded the car ferry for Calais. After this, it stopped being fun. Motoring through France was ineffably boring: long white dusty roads, flat land, endless rows of poplar trees, and the July heat. The rexine seats in the car became so hot that we had to cover them to sit in comfort. My job was to keep reminding Jimmy to keep to the right. I forgot once and we nearly met our death.

Jimmy looked ill. His nerves were in rags. We stopped off at various pensions and I had to use my very bad French to book us in for the night. We were living out of suitcases and our clothes were really messed about. Everywhere we went we seemed to lose something. We dashed through France into Switzerland and had a day and a night to absorb the beauty of Lucerne. How I longed just to stay there but no: off we went over the Swiss Alps through that wonderful tunnel of ice, the St Gotthard Pass. We picnicked in the snow. The sun was warm and with cow-bells tinkling and echoes in the mountains of shepherds herding their sheep and yodelling for their sheep-dogs, it was a veritable fairyland.

In the middle of all this I felt fear; Jimmy looked so ill

and tired. Finally, we came down to the Italian Riviera and beautiful, flower-filled Alassio. Joy of joys: we were to stay there for five days, and so were able to unpack and relax. On the third day as we were returning from the beach, there was a telegram for Jimmy. It read: "Mildred died peacefully yesterday. Funeral Wednesday, Dad." I looked out at the azure blue sea, the happy crowds, and did what I always do when I am told someone has died; I said a little prayer for the journey of her soul.

Too soon we were charging homeward again, the heat once more unendurable, especially at the border checkpoints where streams of cars queued for two to three hours. The only thing that cheered us up was the promise of two days in Paris. We spent a day in Monte Carlo. I was so disappointed: long stony beaches with stones so hot that we (like everyone else) had to buy cork-soled sandals to walk down to the sea. The beaches were divided into ritzy beach clubs, with bars and showers and even white imported sand. Visitors had to pay ten pounds a day as entrance fee to these exclusive clubs, with a chair and sun umbrella costing extra. In the 1950s it was a very expensive business. Ice-cream was sold by bronzed Romeos who sang out, "'Allo Sophia Loren, 'allo Brigitte Bardot, you buy gelati!" It was £1 for a very minute ice-cream!

Fairly worn out by our drive from the south, we booked into a pension on the outskirts of Paris. It was a strange sprawling house, painted pink and nearly smothered in fig trees. They virtually covered even the windows. We were all so tired we slept like the dead but too early in the morning Wendy burst in to our room. "Mummy, my bed's full of ants!" I jumped up and found that our bed was infested too! They were running everywhere, even into the suitcases, and we were all covered with bites! Breakfast of coffee and croissants was served by Madame la Patronne. I tried to tell her about the ants but she shrugged and laughed. "Voilà: c'est la maison des *ants*," and pointed to the trees. This was where they were coming from. I stirred my coffee. To my horror a large ant was in the cup, swimming for its life. Between fantasy and fact there is sometimes only a very thin dividing line. I looked at Madame. She was hunched over, her bulbous eyes out on stalks. The queen ant? I could imagine it all dissolving into the sandy ground and her with it.

What had we to show for our holiday? Hardly any suntan, a few souvenirs, a glimpse at various countries, five cases full of dirty clothes, and ants!

The very first poem I learned from one of my governesses was Robert Louis Stevenson's "My Shadow." She and I would recite over and over: "I have a little shadow that goes in and out with me/And what can be the use of him is more than I can see." At four years of age I was frightened of the way my shadow followed me. As I grew older, the fear grew worse because I thought my shadow was trying to tell me bad things that might happen. Mother made it worse by saying, "As long as you live, you'll walk with your own shadow." My shadow had much to tell me over the years.

One day Jimmy decided to take Billy fishing. He was fifteen and already a keen angler. Tony, our beloved labrador, went with them. They were going somewhere on the north side of the city. That evening I was working in the kitchen when I got this sudden feeling of shock. I remember clearly that it was 6.30 p.m. A cup I was drying fell and broke, and almost simultaneously the phone rang. It was Jimmy. "I've crashed the car outside the Phoenix Park!" Then typically, "The car's a write-off. I only have a scratch. I'm afraid Billy's teeth are broken; he'll be all right. I'll get home as quick as I can." My mind was in a turmoil— it was all too casual.

At nine o'clock, Jimmy arrived home with a doctor friend, who had called an ambulance and organised everything. Jimmy had come out of the Park at a sharp left turn but someone had taken away the stop sign and the car crashed head-on into a double-decker bus, which in turn knocked down a light standard that fell through the roof of a house. Luckily the occupier was downstairs. The car folded up like a concertina; poor Billy was pitched through the windscreen on to the road. (There were no safety belts in those days). The dog was flung forward and his tail was dripping blood like a wet paint brush. Jimmy said that Billy had jumped up and said, "I'm fine; I want a Club orange." They went into a shop nearby where Billy collapsed. Then Jimmy saw that the muscles of his knee were bulging out. The ignition key had gone through it. An ambulance had taken them to the Adelaide Hospital.

Billy was much worse than I had expected and was heavily sedated. His lovely teeth were all smashed but luckily the knee injury had missed the bone. However, with the good nursing in the Adelaide, he soon started to recover and enjoyed the attention of the pretty nurses. I was praying that he would be home for Christmas, then three weeks away. As soon as I heard that he was going to be discharged, I spent ages getting his room nice and decorating the Christmas tree. When he finally got home he was a bit grumpy. He missed the attention he had got used to in the hospital and remarked how small our Christmas tree was after the one in the hospital. I understood how he felt.

Jimmy's father had taken his Mildred's death very badly. He was one of those people who simply cannot live alone. At the time of her death, he had been a very vigorous eighty, sailing small boats in the bay and still winning trophies. We had given him an eightieth birthday party—all his sailing friends came—and he had played his tin whistle. I remember that as we left to go home Jimmy hugged his Dad and said, "I hope if I live to be eighty, I'll be as good as you." Life can be so intolerably sad. Anyway Grandpa started pestering a good-looking widow with his attentions. At eighty he was all on for a third marriage! He had always liked women and often said of his two marriages, both of which lasted twenty years, that he did not know which one was the happier. Sadly both wives died of cancer.

Aunt Mona, too, posed a problem. She was missing Mother dreadfully, and barely managed to live on the wretched deed of covenant the O'Sullivan family had reluctantly paid into. She lived in a depressing bedsit in Dun Laoghaire and understandably became bitter, and indeed quite wicked! She laid awful curses on people! One of her favourites was: "May so-and-so die rotting with cancer." Even Jimmy, who had been brought up in a non-superstitious ethos, began to be uneasy about her curses. We had had such a lot of incredibly bad luck. Aunt Mona laid the cancer curse on Jimmy because he gave me twenty pounds to buy new clothes. I remember how wicked she looked when she spat out these words; she was a curious mixture of real kindness and something rather evil.

In between troubles, we continued our Sunday outings with the family. Jimmy was a keen angler, and one particular Sunday we headed for a place called Kilbride on the north side of the city. There was a hotel there (since burned down) called the Glen Heste. You turned into a long driveway. On the left was the river with sloping banks and on the other side of the hotel (a long sprawling mansion— a rather awesome and dark place) was a cemetery.

After the morning's fishing was over, we lunched in the hotel, and a chatty waitress told us that the place was haunted. My children were still young: Pauline twelve, Billy ten and little Wendy only four. We walked across a sun-baked field. To the left was an unexpected wooded copse, with yew trees standing like sentinels in a circle. "There's the family grave," Jimmy said. Little Wendy was skipping ahead. Suddenly in a sing-song voice she started to chant: "Isabella, Isabella, Isabella Pratt," as if she was calling someone. "Who's Isabella?" I asked. Her eyes were dreamy, and she did not answer. We walked through the turnstile into what looked like a druid circle. The tall trees shut out the sunlight, the mossy ground felt damp. We all experienced a feeling of chill. In the middle of the circle stood a painted Victorian headstone. I read the inscription: "Here lieth Captain Fitzmaurice Pratt." Underneath was inscribed "his sister Isabella Pratt." How or why had a four-year-old child, who could neither read nor write, made contact. It meant nothing to little Wendy. We decided not to talk about it, although when we got home I found her talking to the painted Victorian lady on a firescreen. She would try to feed her and kept prattling, "Isabella, how are you? Are you all right now?" After a week of this Wendy's game stopped and she never mentioned Isabella Pratt again.

10

GATHERING CLOUDS

Life no longer ran on an even keel. Everything seemed to go wrong. One evening Jimmy telephoned to say that his father had suffered a mild stroke. The Billy Mooney, the Grandpa we all knew and loved, had gone. A childish, insecure old man had taken his place. He would open the door and say, "Come in!" and then shut it in your face. He could not cut up his own food and might walk up the road in his pyjamas. He kept ringing Jimmy at his busy dental practice to tell him he had sold out all his shares, and he did many other crazy things.

(My worry was my husband. Jimmy continued to look ill. He had slipped a disc heaving a heavy mast down at the yacht club. Sometimes I would find him lying flat on the floor to ease the pain.) In every affliction there is (or should be) the saving grace of laughter. One of the things I dreaded was taking Grandpa for a walk. He loved the walks! We would get out on the footpath, me holding his arm, and stroll for a while relatively peacefully. One day as we walked he said (and he always spoke in an objective and most interested manner about his own condition), "People my age incline to stoop or bend over. We suffer from locomotorataxia." Before I could ask what it was, he was off—the two legs running away with him. I grabbed him by the belt in desperation but I could scarcely hold him. We were going down a hill towards Bullock Harbour. I shouted out to some men on a scaffolding, "Help me hold on to this old man, please!" Some of the workmen kindly came to my aid. They had to hold Billy by the two elbows while the legs kept going like mad.

We got him home. Mary, his kindly housekeeper, and her husband, John, who took care of him, stood at the open door of his house, mouths agape at the sight of the old man scuttling between his big minders. They began laughing and soon the whole party was laughing too. The next day the phone rang. "It's Grandpa. It's a lovely day to go for a walk," he said. Sweet God preserve us. Not me! At only seven stone I was too small. John and Mary agreed to take him.

One evening I said to Grandpa, who was sucking his pipe like a baby's soother, "What do you think is wrong with Jimmy?" He looked at me with cunning old eyes and said, "We won't know till they open him up and have a look." I felt a terrible fear come over me.

Grandpa was forever (most cheerfully) discussing his own funeral: "I will be buried with my two wives, Dolly and Mildred, and when the grave has sunk and been filled in again with clay, I want green marble chippings." The strange thing was that he was interested in a very nice woman who used to come and sit with him to give us all some relief. He called her "the babysitter" and would say,

"When I get fit again I'll marry her."

Three months dragged by; we were nearly used to his new and sad senility. Then Mary, the housekeeper, was on the phone. "Mr Mooney looks terrible bad and he's taken all his tablets!" He had anti-coagulant pills to stop his blood clotting and he had been eating them like Smarties. He had turned ashen white and was coughing up blood. So it was coming, another demise. I knew his good-byes would not hurt because his mind was disorientated. Yet it was good-bye to Ardfern, his lovely home sloping down to the sea, good-bye to the conservatory with his grapevines and plants, good-bye to his giant telescope with which he used to watch all the yacht races.

Billy Mooney was not religious but he was a decent and honest man and he brought up his sons in the same way. I wondered what spiritual consolation, if any, he was going to find before he died. His main solace was that the nice young widow, his babysitter, came to see him every day in the hospital. He knew that he was dying and just accepted it. I think he had given up; he didn't want to live alone and he couldn't cope with the loneliness. He was tied in his chair in his hospital room and would say, "I'll see you out to the hall." He thought he was at home.

He continued to talk about his funeral: "I don't want my coffin to go out the back gate; the procession must go out the front gate, the coffin followed by a cortège of cars, first four family." He even chose the hymns, including his favourite, "For Those in Peril on the Sea." One evening Jimmy and I were sitting with him chatting. Grandpa was tucked up in bed for the night. "Who's that girl?" he said, pointing to a picture on the wall. "Saint Teresa," I replied. "She's very pretty." Right up to the end, he liked women.

The next day he kept saying, "I'm going down a dirty big hole in the ground." I felt he was saying this because he was looking for some kind of reassurance. I said, "You're not; you're in for a surprise! You'll wake up on the other side and have to sort out things with your two wives." Finally he had another stroke, and this time he just lay there comatose. I would say to him, "It's Sheila. If you know me, squeeze my hand," and for about a week his fingers squeezed mine. He knew I was there. Dying is a lonely business. At the end Grandpa was a mass of tubes, kept alive by a machine. The doctor said that if he lived, he would be a cabbage. Poor Jimmy had to make the decision: should they pull out the tubes? The following evening, having made his decision, he and I went to the hospital. The evening sun was blazing in the long window. Pretty Sister Marion stood at the top of the stairs in the glow; she looked like an angel. She said to Jimmy, "Your father passed away five minutes ago. I was with him. I held his hand and said a little prayer into his ear."

"Thank you, God," I said, "and thank you that he died with a pretty woman holding his hand."

We saw him in the mortuary, in his clean pyjamas. He looked serene and well enough to be going home. Mother's voice seemed to say to me, "That's it; he is going home."

Vita mutatur non tollitur. (Life is changed not taken away.)

Billy Mooney had the funeral he wanted. The church was packed; people were even standing in the aisles. The flags flew at half mast at the three yacht clubs in Dun Laoghaire. In St Patrick's Church on the hill overlooking the sea at Dalkey his favourite hymn rose and swelled higher. Across the bay a little boat sailed into the sunset.

Once again, a holiday was on the agenda. I said a firm no when taking the car was suggested. Jimmy looked so ill and complained about his back. I asked him to go and have a check-up. The deaths of Mildred and his father had been his excuse for not going. Now he kept saying, "After the holiday." He decided on Benidorm. Pauline and Billy refused to come after the misery of the last trip but Wendy was roped in. I was very apprehensive. Two days before we were due to leave, Jimmy said, "Billy will have to take over and go in my place; my back is too bad." Finally he agreed to come.

We stayed in a lovely hotel overlooking the bay and we spent every day on the beach. It was tremendously hot and I kept in the shade under a beach umbrella. Jimmy turned mahogany brown. I noticed round his shoulders little lumps like knuckles on a clenched fist. "What are those little lumps on your back?"

"Secondaries," he replied.

I felt a cold shiver despite the heat, but dismissed the awfulness of what he had said as part of the depressive and foul humour he had been in since we came away. It was miserable. He did not speak to me unless he had to and kept his back to me in bed. All the package holiday soirées were off—the famous barbecues, flamenco dancing displays and the rest. The waiters in the hotel gave a party to which all the girls flocked, with plenty of loud music and singing!

I felt sorry for Wendy. She was eleven. When you're young, fun on a holiday is a priority.

The dining-room became a nightmare. Waiters would pull out a chair for Jimmy, but he would say, "It's too low" or "too high." One day he said it nine times before we were finally seated. I felt that everyone was looking at us. But he did not say, until we got home, that his back had been giving him hell and he could not sit unless he got a supportive chair. Those lovely flower-scented nights! I was never so unhappy in all my life. Later he told me his silence was due to blinding headaches.

When we arrived home, we discovered that Pauline had got a new job with a Dublin solicitor. She was not going to work for her father any more. Billy was in his last term at school and wondering how he would get a job. It was the end of June 1971 and the economic recession was starting. Billy hated Blackrock College, and through him I hated it too. He was regularly slapped on the hand with a hard leather strap called the biffer by the Holy Ghost Fathers, but when he was threatened by the dean of discipline with a caning of twelve strokes on the behind, we reported it to the dean of the college and took our son away. Billy's crime was mitching from his maths class and being caught reading in the grounds. I am reminded of Bob Geldof's description of his caning in his book *Is That It?* There the dean said he was going to treat him like a dog.

Meanwhile I was nagging Jimmy to go and have a medical check-up. I do not think he would have gone into the hospital but that he got a fright. We were driving back from lunch in Howth. Suddenly the car was zig-zagging in a most alarming way. "What's wrong?" I said.

"I keep getting blurred vision. I must be getting meningitis, or something."

We started off again. There was more zig-zagging and we nearly hit an oncoming car. The next day at work in his dental surgery Jimmy had to down tools, his patient left agape, with his mouth full of cotton wool, because his vision had become totally distorted. Finally, two of his doctor friends hijacked him into the Adelaide Hospital for two days and two nights for tests. Jimmy was always one for self-diagnosis. This time he said to me, "I can tell you what the hospital will find: I have a slipped disc and I am in for a dose of meningitis." Somehow I felt this time it was only his defence mechanism; something was much deeper in the back of his mind.

In hospital he ran the gauntlet of tests. The prime one was a biopsy to remove a small piece of cartilage from his spine which would go to pathology for testing. He also had X-rays—brain-scans especially—to discover the cause of his distorted vision and headaches.

On the afternoon of the following day, I toiled in to the hospital, feeling terribly apprehensive and nervous. When I reached Jimmy's room, I peeped through the glass spyhole in the door. He had had a general anaesthetic for the biopsy and I was expecting to see him lying prone and white-faced. Not so. With his specs on, he was sitting up, thoroughly enjoying the peace of reading his *Irish Times*, and he seemed in very good form. He told me that the X-ray had shown up a shadow on his spine. "It's, I'm sure, only cartilage growing round where I slipped the disc."

Yet, despite his cheerful self-diagnosis, I was not happy. We were told he could go home, but to come back in three days when they would have all the results for us.

When we got home, Jimmy was in better form than he had been for ages. It was July and he could not wait to get out in his boat, a Firefly, *Wendy*, named after our younger daughter. She was his crew and like her father was a natural for sailing. He was very proud of her. In all their races they always came second. He coerced Billy to go with him too. Like me, our son was not a keen sailor but he went out and on that occasion they came in first. Jimmy was delighted.

We returned to the hospital. After a long, tense wait, a nurse came into the waiting-room. "Doctor Mooney? Your surgeon and a doctor from St Luke's [the cancer hospital] will see you now." I would have shot her if I'd had a gun in my hand! I felt sick. Poor Jimmy. Ashen-faced, he said to me, "There you are; there's your answer."

We went to meet the doctors. His surgeon was a friend and a sailing colleague. He introduced the doctor from St Luke's. The surgeon watched me closely. He needn't have. Father's words came back to me: "Remember you are a soldier's daughter." I showed no emotion but the opening words are forever imprinted on my mind.

> Jimmy : Have I cancer?
> Surgeon: Yes, I'm sorry, Jim.
> Doctor from St Luke's: We'll see what we can
> do.

Jimmy was later told (I did not know) that it was utterly

hopeless. He had sarcoma; his spine was gone, finished. The double vision was due to a frontal inter-cranial pituitary brain tumour, on a stalk pressing on the optic nerve. There was another brain tumour at the base of his skull. Jimmy asked bravely, "Am I terminal?"

"Yes—I'm sorry."

"How long have I got?"

"About eight months."

That day in July, his hell, mine, our son's and daughters' began. His eyes had the look of a condemned man. He turned his back on life and had started to die. Billy had now to chauffeur Jimmy. He could no longer drive because of the double vision in his left eye. So we went silently to the bank to arrange for me to draw cheques in his name; then to the building society. The managers of both establishments looked bemused at the tension and silence and I could not intervene. When we got home it was worse. There was no talking. The treatment was to be given every afternoon in the hospital which was fifteen miles away. Meanwhile, Jimmy, with a patch over one eye, was going to work for as long as he could every morning. Some mornings he had cobalt treatment and was driven home for lunch by Billy and back in the afternoon for more treatment. Then he had to employ a locum, and poor Billy had to drive his father in to Dublin and out twice a day at about 20 mph. No bumps were allowed in case one of Jimmy's spinal vertebrae would collapse and cause untold agony. His spine was like a rotten and brittle branch.

Jimmy did not speak to me at all and I felt terrible. What had I done? How could I be blamed? At the end of one week's silence, one night when Jimmy was climbing painfully into bed (we had a board under the mattress), I said these inadequate words: "I am so very sorry." He turned and looked at me and said, "You always gave me too much tinned food." I was amazed and then I laughed for nearly twenty minutes. So I was to be the whipping boy. "Show your courage to the world; keep your tears to yourself!" And that is what I did for the eight months of his dying.

The treatment was hell for Jimmy. It meant nausea, endless vomiting and dry retching. He would lie on the settee in the darkened sitting-room for hours with a handkerchief over his eyes. One morning I awoke and all the pillows were covered in hanks of thick black hair. I wept, "Jimmy, Jimmy, your hair's falling out." He sat up and laughed: "Here's some more," and he tugged out a handful. He was soon as bald as an egg. I used to see men, women and the dear little children in the hospital—bald, with blue crosses to spot where the cobalt or radium would pinpoint the cancer. One particular day stands out in my mind. I opened the hall door on hearing the car and Jimmy stumbled in, supported by Billy on one side and by our family doctor on the other. Jimmy had a cut on his forehead. He had fallen in the surgery. A woman appeared at our gate and in a beastly shrill English voice shouted, "Will you be able to do my teeth for me, Jimmy? I'd just hate the idea of going to someone else." I wanted to shout out, "Damn you and damn your bloody teeth!"

11

THE DYING OF THE YEAR

It was a beautiful summer, our last summer together; the sun shone every day, and joy of joys, Jimmy went into remission. We used to sit out in the garden in the big canopied swing-chair and all his sailing friends came to see him. That's the nearest to being happy he got in those last eight months, talking about his great love, boats and the sea. We decided we were experiencing everything for the first time: the colour of the flowers, the joy of the little birds, the companionship of our children.

But by September Jimmy was rapidly going downhill and sadly the last blooming of our marriage began. With great sadness he sold his dental practice, then his new car. Finally his boat, because Wendy, then only thirteen, had not enough ballast to sail it on her own. There was a wonderful gesture of kindness from a patient who had heard about the boat; a piano arrived from Mr Walton (of Waltons) the day the boat was taken away. I will always remember people's kindness during those terribly dark days.

Jimmy stayed out of bed up to the last month. The spirit was forever willing. One day to my horror he shuffled out to the garage.

"What are you going to do?" I asked him.

"Scrape the rust off the kitchen window frames."

I was inside the kitchen at the sink and there he was, one eye covered, scraping away. Suddenly his hand slipped and he cracked the glass. Neither of us said a word and I watched as he painfully dragged the ladder back to the garage. He never tried any household chores again.

Jimmy had always been highly strung, though he kept it under control. As his cancer progressed there were only certain people he could easily converse with. If anyone made him tense he could feel quite sick within five minutes. So when a visitor arrived I would ask, "Jimmy, can you see so and so?" The answer was either "No!" or "I would love to see him/her." I understand exactly how he felt; when I am well, there are people who make me feel sick. This was a man with two brain tumours.

I could never say to him, "How are you?" or "Any better?" because we both knew that he was dying. The worst cloud on the horizon was the fact that our last Christmas was coming and I would have to play the awful game of "Let's pretend." I had to do the best I could for our son and two daughters. I hoped they would be asked out to a few parties. It was not to be. Billy, like me, was on duty all the time, driving and waiting about in hospital for his father. Poor Jimmy was covered with blue crosses on his head and body. Coming up to December 1971, he was a walking skeleton, his suits hanging off him. One day in the hospital waiting-room, a man came in. Like Jimmy he was bald and thin, wore an eye-patch and leant heavily on his stick. Jimmy and the man exchanged glances and then recognised each other.

"It's Jimmy, by God! Some place to meet!"

"And you, Ray—the same as me?"

They were old friends and one-time sailing colleagues. Both of them were now dying. Later I saw a letter Ray wrote to Jimmy:

I too am terminal and time is running out. Let's drink a toast to the good times we've known and when we go down let the old flag be flying at the mast head!

Men with that spirit are the real heroes.

I began to notice a change: Jimmy accepted his dying, yet at the same time clung to life as hard as he could. As in a VCR I would turn on my memories of the past—all my yesterdays. Remembering the balls, with Mother always the star of the show, kept me sane. In Saintbury we had a coal scuttle and a basket for turf. Jeff, the tortoise, liked the heat and he would often crawl into the turf basket. Mother was a great one for keeping the fire blazing and would periodically throw on a log of turf. One night she chucked what she thought was a log of turf on to the fire but it was really Jeff. Luckily I grabbed him quickly and, as he drank his milk later that night, we all were delighted to see that the poor thing was none the worse for his terrible experience. I really could write an entire book and call it *Remembering Mother*. There was no one like her. Thinking of her while Jimmy was so ill helped me and even made me laugh. Perhaps she was near to me and trying to support me.

When my father was dying of pneumonia, Mother said,

"I've given up cigarettes to save your father's life." She was an inveterate smoker. About half an hour later I went into her room and she was puffing away. She laughed nervously. "Isn't it awful!" she said. "I'll just have to let him go." Maybe there was some sort of a lesson for me in remembering that black remark. The words: "I'll just have to let him go" now applied to me, a fool of a woman, who never stopped believing that a miracle would happen.

Jimmy's brain tumours were not affecting his mind; his brain was as alert as ever and he had all his affairs in apple-pie order. A new and rather depressing subject had cropped up: Christian burial, Jimmy's and mine! Since he was Church of Ireland and I Roman Catholic, we could not be buried together. In Ireland there is still segregation. There is a Protestant and a Catholic quarter and never the twain shall meet. I do not wish to be buried with anyone! Mother refused to be buried with Father; she said that she couldn't bear the thought of their bones eventually mingling. Jimmy went on and on about "our" burial and sent a friend to the local cemetery to enquire whether it was possible. The answer was no, and secretly I was pleased. All I want of my inconsequential mortal remains is that perhaps my old bones will make a little patch of grass that much greener. Mother used to say, "There'll be no peace in the world until all the churches are shut!" Maybe she was not so far wrong.

Quite a number of Catholic priests called to see Jimmy and, contrary to opinion and rumour, they did not try to convert him. Their conversations were mostly about fishing, shooting and football. He was always glad to see them.

People of their calling know how to deal with the sick and they never stayed too long. Looking back I remembered happier times when I had always made Christmas lunch for Mother and Aunt Mona, but that was all over. Now I had no choice but to keep up the façade of Christmas and buy cards and presents.

There would be only myself and my children to sit down and eat the dinner. Jimmy, I knew, would eat nothing. The tree was dressed and we had taken it in turns to go to church because Jimmy could not be left alone. I cannot remember what the children gave him for Christmas. For some time the awful dilemma had been on my mind: what present do you give a dying man?

He was distressed that he could not go out and buy us presents. I think he gave me the money to buy them. Presents were the last thing on my mind. Jimmy had taken to bed and every afternoon he was so weak that he had to be propped up with pillows in the car. A porter would come out with a wheelchair to take him into the hospital. A couple of friends joined us for Christmas dinner. We were having pre-dinner drinks. Jimmy, I thought, was asleep upstairs but the door opened and there he was, fully dressed in his best suit, with a new tie and matching handkerchief in breast pocket. The suit was just hanging off him.

"I thought I'd come down and join the party," he said bravely.

Within ten minutes he had collapsed and we had to get him back up to bed. He had made such a courageous effort, it broke my heart. Christmas was hardly gone before I started to dread New Year's Eve. It used always be our very happy night out. We went to the dance in the yacht club in Dun Laoghaire and I made sure I had a new dress. By the time that New Year's Eve arrived, Jimmy had failed so much that I kept asking his doctor how much longer did they think he had.

I insisted that the children all go out to see in the New Year. For me, it turned out to be even worse than I had expected. I had planned to take a couple of sleeping pills and knock myself out before the local church bells rang in the New Year. I did not want to hear the ships' hooters, people dancing in the street, or the folk at the party across the road sing "Auld Lang Syne." So I took my pills and crept into bed beside my sleeping husband. He was heavily sedated on Largactil. I always slept on the very edge of the bed, practically on the bedside table, so as not to disturb him.

I fell into an exhausted sleep but woke because everything felt wet, right up to the back of my neck. I switched on the light. It was 3 a.m. Jimmy had wet the bed. He was out for the count. I felt so alone; everyone was out. I dismissed my feeling of sheer panic. I tried to remember what a nurse (usually two of them) would do. With great difficulty I rolled the wet sheet out from under him, and, sweating, changed his pyjamas. Equally arduous was getting the dry sheet rolled under him. I put towels under and around him, washed and changed myself. Then I went to the kitchen and left the wet sheets steeping. Exhausted, I stumbled back into the bed.

Happy, happy bloody New Year!

Next day I washed the sheets by hand; I had no washing machine. I hung them out. There was a bitter wind and the wet sheets lashed my face. It was awful but I had no time to cry. When everything was over, I would allow myself that indulgence. My health and strength were beginning to suffer. I could leave the bedroom only when Jimmy was under sedation. I would often just be trying to eat a bit of food when I would hear him. We had fixed up an intercom and he would either be calling me or banging a walking stick against the wall. Once I wasn't quick enough and he had wet the bed. He would say, "That's no way to treat a patient." I felt terrible.

My weight was down to nearly six stone but I had to go on. I had so much time to think while sitting in Jimmy's darkened bedroom. Ours was a house with no laughter, but sometimes remembering could make me laugh. I recalled a time when Grandpa, fit and well and married to his plump Mildred, had called up to the house cheerfully sucking his empty pipe. "Where's Jimmy?" he said.

"In the garage, working on bits of his boat," I replied.

Later I heard the two of them coming into the house. Grandpa said, "Would you have such a thing as a roll of bandage?"

"I have. What for?" Jimmy asked.

"Will you come along with me and help me tie up Nellie's jaw."

Nellie was Billy's sister who had just died. The wicked thought crossed my mind: her jaw would have been better tied up while she was alive! The two of them drove off jovially together. They were hard men and it took a lot to move them.

I used to muse in that darkened room. My head was so full of memories because I could not see any tomorrows without Jimmy and I did not want to think about the vista of lonely years stretching ahead of me. Mercifully, our doctor fitted Jimmy with a catheter so that we had a dry bed. He ate nothing except a little Complan and drank Ribena. A strange and lovely thing happened to him during his last sickness. He had been born tone deaf; as he said, he could not tell "Pop Goes the Queen" from "God Save the Weasel!" But suddenly he began to love music and asked me to put a small transistor near his ear. He listened during all his conscious moments to a new world of music and he would go to sleep with peace on his face.

One of Jimmy's favourite sayings was: "Never laugh at the village fool. He is the happy man with no worries." I would look over to the bed at my dying husband, recalling our honeymoon in London when we lived like millionaires for a short while, even though my father had cut me out of his life and his will and none of my family came to the wedding except Mother. I thought of how we had danced the night away in the Savoy and the Dorchester, once performing an exhibition samba to a great round of applause. Bring back the music; bring back the memories: the incredible joy of seeing my newborn babies, little angel faces looking up at me. I would not have missed that for anything. I believe that the consummation of the perfect love is the child.

Towards the end, a neighbour said to me, "If you want a miracle, why don't you take your husband to Lourdes?" I answered, "I would not bring Jimmy to Lourdes, he would have to say to me he wanted to go." He never expressed that wish, and we did not discuss religion or life after death.

One evening Jimmy asked me, "What are you always writing?" I was setting down memories and writing poetry to while away the endless hours. I said, "It's about Mother in America."

He had always found Mother incredibly funny, though she could drive him crazy too. To my amazement he said, "Read it to me."

"OK," I said, "and this is the way she told it to me."

I have called it "Mother's visit to Aimée Semple McPherson's Temple."

Mother had been baptised a Catholic, and since she did not like the church's teaching on hell, fire and purgatory, she dabbled in Christian Science. Mother was always perusing Mary Baker Eddy's books *Key to the Scriptures* and *A Divine Healing*. On one of her many visits to the United States to be with my sister, the actress Maureen O'Sullivan, Mother went off with her friend Mrs Pollard to visit the temple where that great show woman, Aimée Semple McPherson, the founder of the Foursquare Gospel Movement, conducted her services. Charter buses thronged the forecourt of the huge marble temple and there were cars parked for miles around.

The interior was lavishly decorated with floral arrangements. The backdrop was a glittering stage-setting with magnificent cloth-of-gold curtains. To the right was a huge organ, to the left was the choir robed in white with long red cloaks. Celestial music played as the enormous congregation took their seats. Then there was a fanfare of trumpets. Spotlights shone down on Aimée McPherson, an ample, well-endowed woman in a long white robe with arms outstretched, the folds of her gown arranged like wings. She had very long blonde hair. Mother said she looked like an archangel, and then ruined it by saying she could do with Bile Beans, to reduce her weight.

The theme of Aimée's homily was the peace that passeth understanding. Mother said that when she was speaking, there was total silence. She had a following akin to Billy Graham's. She knew her Bible and adapted it to the concepts of her own brand of religion. Mother said you could have heard a pin drop. Aimée told the congregation that the divine mind knoweth no imperfection. Hence all sickness is "matter" and man must rise above it and know that it does not exist. Once the truth is known and the patient has the surety that God knows no imperfection, the healing begins. Jimmy interrupted here by saying, "Great advice for a bad toothache." I read on. After her homily Aimée disappeared behind the gold curtains. There was more soft music, then a nasal voice, loudly amplified, asked "my brothers and sisters to be generous." A silent collection was about to take place to "keep this temple a beautiful temple!" Aimée's angels, long-haired girls in white gowns, flitted among the audience gathering the collection!

Then bugles blared out. The gold curtains swished back again and a procession of pages stepped out dressed in medieval costume and carrying tall, lighted candles. The spotlights picked out Aimée again and she announced that the healing of the sick would now begin. The choir started

up the hymn, "Reach Out and Touch the Lord." Slowly up
the aisle a procession wound its way. Cripples on crutches,
the sick, the halt and the blind. Helped by Aimée's angels,
they painfully mounted the stage. The nasal amplified voice
called for: "Silence everybody; silence please." This was
followed by a thunderous roll of drums and then, with
arms outstretched, Aimée announced that she would pray
for a healing for the sick. Mother said that this was not a
silent healing. Aimée bellowed to the heavens, "You just
come right down now, Lord! Right down and let these folk
know that they have risen above mortal belief; they know
that there is no sickness. Heal them Lord! Heal them!"

There were shouts of "Hallelujah! Hallelujah!" The
cripples danced; crutches were thrown into the congregation; the blind saw; wheelchairs were thrown over.
There was holy chaos! Mother said that she got the awful
feeling that the sick were old lags, used for the game. The
healing over, the curtains were closed and the angels
mingled with the audience selling books and leaflets. At
the end the nasal amplified voice intoned, "Sister Aimée is
now going to present gifts to the audience as a memento
of your visit to the temple!"

Back swished the curtains, and on came the medieval
pages dragging large baskets full of gifts. Aimée emerged,
dipped into the hampers and proceeded to fire the presents
into the audience. Mother said that some of the presents
were extraordinary. A man caught two packets of bird seed
and she herself was hit on the head with two pounds of
beef steak. The show over, the crowd pushed their way
towards the exits. In the rush to get out, a crippled woman

gave Mother a crack on the leg with her crutch and mother gave her a good punch back. All this to the strains of the hymn, "Make Me a Channel of Your Peace."

That is how she told her story to me.

12

SUNSET AND EVENING STAR

Jimmy's bedroom was kept in semi-darkness because of his distorted vision and terrible headaches. His life as January 1972 approached could be described only as a hell on earth. I prayed for the good Lord to take him in his sleep— something I thought I would never ask for.

I spent the hours when he slept (under sedation) writing memoirs, remembering, feeling Mother's presence very keenly, and I had the strong feeling that she was desperately worried about me. There were two problems to be faced: Jimmy and myself. I knew that I was going downhill; there was no time to eat proper meals and I suffered greatly from lack of sleep, plus the endless washing of bed linen, well-meaning callers, a phone that rang and rang. And the constant strain of never admitting that he was going to die. On looking back, I don't know how I kept going.

A new and terrible problem was bed sores. Billy and I turned Jimmy as often as we could but he was so emaciated that it hurt him to move. One day he screamed as I put the hot water bottle at his feet. Shaken, I checked that it was not too hot, but I looked in horror at the sores on his heels. His bones were almost protruding, so we had to make pathetic nests of cotton wool for his heels. Jimmy's fifty-first birthday was due on 24 February. I wondered if he would live to see it.

In the afternoons we had the horrendous task of rolling him in a blanket, before a very strong friend carried him down the stairs (still in his pyjamas) and out to the car, laying him on the back seat *en route* to the hospital for treatment. I had no feelings, only numbness and the drive to go on. The strange thing, even then, was that I still believed I would get a miracle. The Protestant clergyman called every day. When he was conscious Jimmy still fussed about our being buried together.

On the birthday there was a small party consisting of myself, our three children and John the gardener whom Jimmy was very fond of. We opened a bottle of champagne. He took a few sips and said, "What are we celebrating?" I replied, "Just us all being together with you." No one dared to say "Happy Birthday." A close friend phoned to ask if I would like her to send Canon Camier, a warm-hearted and jolly man, a lifelong friend of the Mooneys. The canon arrived. Jimmy was unconscious, but he prayed over him. The next day a strange thing happened. In his old strong voice, Jimmy said, "I want to be buried a Catholic, for the family's sake." I said to him, "We are proud of you the way you are; you're better than any of us, especially me." But he was adamant, and he had just had the last rites of his own church! I was nearly dead myself because I had stopped eating; my sight was blurred and all my bones were aching. I was only six stone in weight and so thin I had to kneel in the bath because it hurt to sit.

Towards the end of February, Jimmy was sinking fast. Amazingly, his brain (with two malignant tumours) was perfect. Too weak to speak, he could manage only to whisper. Billy was marvellous, always understanding what his father wanted. I have to admit that at times I could not. He could barely swallow, so I used to dip my finger in Ribena and let him suck the moisture. On 26 February he became very agitated and at 9.30 p.m. was asking for a friend, a patient whom I had never met. A kindly doctor went off in his car and finally tracked down the priest at a golf-club dinner. When he arrived, I unplugged the intercom and shut the bedroom door. What was said between the two men I shall never know. But at no time did the priest try and proselytise. A nasty rumour went about that I had forced Catholicism on my husband when he was over-susceptible. All we gave was love, compassionate love. I never wanted to convert him. Even if I had wanted to, I was too exhausted to try.

After about twenty minutes, the priest came down and said, "He wants to make his First Holy Communion with you and the children." I went into the bedroom. Jimmy's eyes were very bright and alert. He could only barely swallow, but the priest broke the host into tiny bits and told me to wet it with Ribena. Jimmy was just able to get it down. "The Body of Christ. Amen"—so be it. Then Jimmy kissed me and that last kiss had more punch in it than the first! Such strength! He said, "I love you."

Then I saw in a sad blinding flash my miracle. In those terrible eight months we had gone through together, our marriage had reached its greatest heights. "For better, for worse till death." I said to him, "I love you." He answered, "I know that." Almost immediately he sank into a coma. He never spoke again. That night I slept beside him. His breathing was getting worse. Billy came into the room, and I said to him, "It's our last night together." He nodded. We both knew our job was nearly over. The following day the house was full of people who did not matter: I was too tired to care. At 10.30 that night the priest was sent for. This was the finale—my husband was going to die. Only the three of us were in the room. Hearing is the last of the senses to go and, to my eternal regret, I did not speak into his ear at the last. But the well-meaning priest sat beside him reading his prayer book while I knelt and watched. The breathing was distressing, but his beautiful hands were loosely folded and relaxed and I knew he was not suffering. A little gurgling sound come from his throat. The priest said, "He is going now, alanna." I fell to my knees and covered my eyes. "*Profiscere, anima Christiana, de hoc mundo.*" (Depart, O Christian soul, from this life.) He did not linger. I was aware of his spirit leaving that room.

What was in the bed had no significance. I switched on the light and opened the drawer to look for a pair of black gloves. Nature provides her own anaesthesia. I felt nothing. I turned off the light and left the room. As I shut the door, I said to our son, "That's it. Our job is done." I went downstairs where the priest was now talking to relations and friends. I sat down, I felt they all expected me to cry, but I was exhausted and felt nothing. We talked of everything except what had happened. A knock came to the door. A pretty girl stood there. "Mrs Mooney, I feel embarrassed and I do apologise, but I was sent to do the laying-out. That will be fifteen pounds please." I thanked her and gave her the cheque, without showing any emotion.

The family and I went upstairs, along with Jimmy's dear friend and doctor. What I said when I looked across at the bed remains forever in my mind. I said, "That is not my Jimmy." There was no resemblance to the man I had known. His month's growth of beard had been shaved away and a fuzz of iron grey hair had replaced the thick black mop he had once had. The appalling regalia the firm of undertakers had provided as a shroud was an insult. If it were possible to ridicule the dead, this was it. There was a cheap white paper shroud with a large and garish picture of the Sacred Heart on it. His chin was propped up with a crucifix belonging to Mother, used without my permission, his poor thin arms and legs stuck out, making him look so pitiful. It was an insult to the Protestant he had been all his life, and to Roman Catholicism. We do have some finesse! Had I been less weary, I would have insisted they change him into a suit of pyjamas. I could not pray beside my husband's remains that night because I was so convinced from the moment of his passing that what was left was only an empty shell.

That night I slept in the living-room or rather talked half the night with my son. Gulliver, the hamster, kept up his nocturnal habit and went round and round on his wheel. Pauline and Wendy were sharing a bedroom upstairs. I thought how strange is life: my husband and their father lying dead in his bed. We had known him so well, but because he was now a corpse we were all a little afraid. Perhaps it is because we have to come to terms with our own mortality. The morning came, and with it, friends to pay their respects. Neighbours drew their curtains as a mark of respect. I did appreciate the gesture. One of the many things I love about Irish people is their great consideration for the dead and the bereaved.

This day held that awesome business, the removal of remains to the church for an overnight vigil. In the afternoon at 4.30 two men arrived with the coffin and we were all summoned to the bedroom. I simply could not take it in. I looked in the coffin. They had put a stupid piece of gauze over his face. I angrily threw it to the floor. I kissed his forehead and then bravely started the "Our Father" but I broke down and could not go on. A cousin of Jimmy's said some nice informal prayer. Lessing, the German playwright wrote, "There are things in life which must cause you to lose your reason or you would have none to lose."

There were crowds at the church, including all his sailing friends, and the mortuary chapel was full of flowers and mass cards: the trappings of death. Two decades of the rosary were recited for the repose of Jimmy's soul, he who had been Church of Ireland all of his life up to three days before his death. I don't suppose he ever gave a thought in life to a "Hail Mary." I thought of Wendy and her description of the Mother of God at the foot of Her son's cross. She was not the wimpy woman with bowed head. Wendy wrote about her, "The Virgin Mary raised her head and screamed." That I could identify with.

A local character, a hunchback who was to be seen at every funeral, started flustering around, mumbling and blessing herself. "Who is it then, God rest him?" She had one foot in a high boot because of a club foot. I heard a loud crack and realised that the old woman had walked on our beautiful family wreath and had broken it with her foot. Almost immediately I seemed to hear Mother's voice, "If I was there, I'd have given her a punch and put her out." I will always remember that as our cortège passed down the road, a neighbour, an old soldier who was walking his dog, stood to attention, hat on chest as the coffin passed. He was paying his tribute to a brave man.

I took sleeping pills that night and slept an exhausted sleep akin to death. The next day was the funeral. I woke with Father's last words to me ringing in my ears: "I hope you'll be happy, but I don't think you will." Well he was wrong. We had our ups and downs, but for twenty-three years there was no messing about and with three lovely children so much to be thankful for.

The day was cold but at least it was not raining. The church was crowded. The old parish priest apologised to me because he could not be there for the last blessing, as was his habit; he had been called somewhere else. I looked at him dully. How could he possibly think I would have noticed his presence or his absence. Another nitwit of a priest came over and said, "You must be glad it ended happily." I felt annoyed when I got the gist of what he meant: a conversion—"one for us!" I felt like saying something, but a church is not the place. Strangely, on that funeral day it was Father's words that kept coming to me, not Mother's. He used say, "You'll have to harden up; you'll have to try and be harder. Don't be a squealer. Show your courage to the world; keep your tears to yourself!" I did exactly that, as we followed the coffin down the aisle, resolving that I had the rest of my life to cry.

Poor Billy looked tired. For eight months he had worked so hard and so lovingly and at the end of it all he had lost his Dad. I remembered how proud her father had been about Pauline, our first-born; how he took the tiny baby in her carrycot down to the yacht club to show her off to his friends. He was proud too of Wendy. "She's great in the boat," he'd say. He really loved his children. My friends from long ago had come along to give me their love and support. It was touching, too, to see Wendy's class from the Holy Child in Killiney lined up outside the church.

I had been asked if I wanted a first or a second-class grave. The first-class plots were nearer to the main gates, the second overlooked a sprouting council estate. Paupers' graves were next to the wall, with just numbers marking the plot. Even a man's bones will be subject to class distinction. Bewildered as I was and short of money, I decided that my husband would be buried in a second-class plot. I felt his mortal remains should have gone to the sea he loved so much. However, the more one believes in life after death, the less these things matter. Looking into that dark grave, at that awesome moment I remembered how many times at funerals Jimmy had quipped, "That's it—six foot down."

I watched as the coffin was lowered. Someone put a very strong arm around me and held me tightly. How much the human touch can mean. The priest gave the last blessing and intoned, "I am the resurrection, and the life: he that believeth in Me, though he were dead, yet he shall live." I thought: What did we do that was so bad to deserve this? I seemed to see Jimmy running away from me. He turned and said, "Ask your father about it."

"About what?"

"Getting married." That had been twenty-three years ago—he was gone. A cold wind was getting up. I buttoned the collar on my black funeral coat, and walked to the waiting car.

13

COPING ALONE

Returning home was very strange. Everything seemed the same. Gypsy, Jimmy's setter, ran out, barking, to greet us. Susan, my help and dear friend, had prepared a lunch for us. A bereavement leaves a print of tragedy on older people's faces. Billy, Pauline and Wendy were too young to show this mark on them and I knew that grief would pass more quickly for them than for me because of the resilience of youth. Here I was, actually sitting down at a table eating a meal and knowing that I would not be disturbed. I still did not feel anything, but I had a distant inner fear of what it would be like when I did. I noticed that the intercom was still on and got up hastily and unplugged it in case I might imagine I heard Jimmy calling me.

There were things to be faced. I had to go up to the empty bedroom even though I dreaded it. Susan had changed the bed linen and all the bottles of pills and various accoutrements were gone. I felt a compulsion to open drawers and the wardrobe. Seeing all his clothes, including his green Olympic blazer, something akin to pain stirred within me. I was so afraid that I was going to have to come to terms with a terrible grief.

I know that no one can feel another's pain and have always hated the stupid assumption of "I know how you feel." But I am fairly sure that one has a better chance of working through a bereavement if one's physical health is good. Everyone knows that body and mind work in unison. I was very badly run-down and had gone from seven and a half stone to six in the eight months. Léon Bloy wrote: "Man has places in his heart which do not yet exist and into there enters suffering in order that they may have existence."

Our financial affairs were in a mess. Jimmy had left his affairs in the once capable hands of his father's solicitor, a charming but very old and confused lady. She had a dusty old-fashioned office and kept her files on the floor. All she could say to me was: "You will find it very hard to manage; things are in a bad way." Unfortunately Miss Sands was too friendly; she would ask us to tea and forget to, or choose not to, deal with anything to do with the practicalities. Her Victorian, high-walled house was guarded by Jamie, the biggest German shepherd I have ever seen. The polite tea-parties continued and she kept sending me mass cards for Jimmy. I was getting frantic. A friend advised me to go to a younger solicitor, who had sold a house for Jimmy while he was ill. I composed a letter to Miss Sands, telling her that for the family's sake I felt a younger solicitor was needed. I tried my best not to hurt her but it was unavoidable. The problem now at hand was to get the papers and documents from Miss Sands. She would promise to send on everything but then didn't. Eventually my new solicitor sent his clerk out to her home to collect the file but he could not get near the house because she let her German shepherd loose and the poor man had to run for his life. Still, eventually we retrieved the necessary papers.

My doctor decided that I needed a holiday. Pauline and Wendy chose a Spanish resort called Lloret del Mar. I did not want to go; I did not feel well enough. The day we left I got the most crucifying pains in my stomach at the airport after our luggage had gone through. I was all for going home but Billy, who was seeing us off, made me get on the plane. The stewardess gave me something when we took off and I felt a little better.

In the hotel I noticed people glance at me and then look away. I had to sit by the swimming-pool on folded towels I was so thin. A friend later told me, "You looked like one of those women repatriated from Belsen or Dachau." I had to bring a rubber ring for ease in sitting everywhere, even into the dining-room. The hotel was terribly impersonal; it was like a huge air terminal. One good thing about the trip was that Pauline and Wendy had a great time. There were plenty of young people for them. After all they had been through, it was good to see them enjoy life again. The holiday did me some good; I felt better able to come to terms with my great loss.

We were hardly home from our holiday when more dark clouds appeared on the horizon. The nuns telephoned from St Monica's, in Belvedere Please Dublin, to say that Miss Frazer had gone into a general hospital for a checkup. Her doctor was anxious about her weight loss and persistent cough. The news when it came was bad: she had a cancer growth in one lung and the other was showing a malignancy too. I went in to see her; she was having difficulty breathing but hated her oxygen mask. We got her a pretty fan, which she preferred. She said, "My word, it reminds me of China." She started to tell me of her love affairs when she was a girl: "I was going to get married, but Mother was ill and I couldn't leave her." Going over the past, seeing it like a fast-forwarded video, seems to be a part of dying.

I have said before that Grandmother Frazer was as strong as a bull and wanted to keep Aunt Mona as her companion-cum-help. Aunt Mona showed me the VAD medals she had got for nursing throughout World War I and asked me to keep them, along with the posthumous citation that her eldest brother Jack was awarded for saving my father's life at the battle of the Somme. He was a member of the First Battalion, the Connaught Rangers, and had been buried in Flanders. Whatever faults the Frazers had, they were a bold, beautiful and bizarre connection—and they were brave.

Aunt Mona suddenly asked me in a purely practical way, "Am I dying?" Because the time was right, I said, "Yes, you are." She answered, "Funny, it's not half as bad as it's made out."

I looked at her, a wasted old lady. Seeing the big hollows in her neck, it was hard to believe she had once been so attractive, vibrant and witty. Yet her eyes, already dimming, remained that beautiful pure blue. She had loved children all her life and yet was destined to have none. Mother had borne the children, but did not care too much about them. I wondered if Aunt Mona knew about the cancer. The

Frazers had a horror of it and always boasted that there had never been cancer in the family. I went to kiss her, but she said, "No, don't come near me," and I realised she had chosen to believe that she had tuberculosis, which the family considered much less offensive. She had become friendly with a very nice Jesuit priest and he had brought her "peace at the last."

Aunt Mona had kept her sense of humour. She dreaded visits from her niece, Betty Frazer, the daughter of Major Edward, second eldest of the brothers. Betty, well-meaning, was nevertheless heavy going and very argumentative. Someone said, "Betty Frazer wants to see you." Mona replied, "Oh! my God, don't let her in. I'll die that much quicker." She said as I was leaving, "Come back tomorrow." The next day I could see that she was failing, though she was very cross and not a bit sanctimonious. "Give me my glasses," she said. I wondered what for. "No, no, for God's sake! the reading glasses." I gave them to her. She said, "I must look awful without my teeth." Her dentures no longer fitted. She asked the nice little nun who nursed her for a sleeping pill, a signal for the family to go. "There you are, dear; your hands are very cold." The nun tucked her hands under the bedclothes. Aunt Mona said, "Can I have another sleeping pill?"

"Yes, dear." Aunt Mona gave me a penetrating look and said, "I'm going to go to heaven." Then she said, "I'll see Jimmy in heaven," and breathed her last very gently. "She's gone," said Sister Agnes. "May the Lord have mercy on her soul."

At the time of her death, money was short and I was

worried about the funeral bill. We decided to bury her with Mother, who if she knew would have forty fits; she hated the idea of bones eventually mingling. I looked at the face of my dead Aunt Mona the next day. She was in life an unusual, bizarre, witty and terrible woman, who adored children. She would curse you to hell one minute and then the next would give you the coat off her back. She did not look serene in death but very grim, as if she was going to come back to haunt someone she did not like. I felt an intruder in the bedroom, where a clutter of old women were crowded round her bed mumbling the rosary. "I am her niece," I said apologetically. The nuns had provided the shroud. Again, like poor Jimmy's, it was just awful—made of paper, white striped with a ruffle collar.

That night I had an awful nightmare that I had died and was gazing at a line of worn-looking people all wearing terrible shrouds walking through enormous open gates. I was perplexed at the paradox of the deference the Irish show to their dead and their tasteless practice of dressing them in dreadful paper shrouds for the finale. To me it's like the song "Send in the Clowns."

There were five of us attended Aunt Mona's lonely funeral. Pauline had left home and gone to work in London. Hence our party consisted of the priest, my younger sister, Wendy and Betty Frazer. We could not afford a shiny funeral limo, so everyone had to squash in my sister's small car. I was nominated to drive in the hearse. It was dark and raining heavily.

The requiem mass was held in St Monica's. All the old ladies, her friends, were there. I could not help thinking that each of them must wonder whose turn might be next. Wendy read the lesson. Aunt Mona would have liked that. I have noticed over and over again—and I mean no disrespect—that to every funeral in Ireland, there is a funny side. My sister drove off with her loaded car while the priest and I sat squashed in the front of the hearse with the driver. We kept passing people I knew and they looked amazed. It would not have been correct to wave. The driver said, "You will be one of the few people who can truly say, 'I enjoyed my drive in the hearse out to the graveyard!'"

We drove into the cemetery and stopped opposite Mother's grave, the rain pouring down. I hoped the priest would not go on for too long but I need not have worried: he was just as anxious as we were not to get soaked in the few moments we stood round the grave, now full of muddy water. They lowered the casket with an awful bump. Stupidly I said, "Oh mind her head." It was not until the car drove away that it hit me: Aunt Mona had gone from us. It's a certainty we shall not see her like again. For some time after her death, I was nervous at night. Although she had died as she had begun, a Roman Catholic, she always delved into spiritualism. I remember her telling of a spiritualists' meeting in the Royal Albert Hall in London. Out of a huge audience, the medium picked on Aunt Mona. "The lady in the fourth row with the green hat, there is a message coming through for you, from your sister Edith: she says she drowned herself because she was too upset at little sister Una dying of tuberculosis but she is happy now and they are together." Witnesses at the meeting confirm that story to be true.

14

NURSE MOONEY

Jimmy's father had left his house in Sandycove to his eldest son Bob and to Jimmy the house in Upper Fitzwilliam Street where he and Jimmy had both practised dentistry. That house proved to be the bane of my life and the tenants, with one exception, a nest of hornets. Billy, and then Jimmy, had no problems with them but now a woman had taken over. The tenants wanted this, that and the other done. The old Georgian houses on this street were built in the days before damp courses; there was no felt under the roof tiles and that bogey, dry rot, kept taking hold. For that, there is no financial comeback. The house required capital for its upkeep; I had none. I also had a couple of "controlled" tenants, one paying me £1 per week, another £5.

It was getting me down; the little money I had was being sucked into that big house for a miserable return income. A friend of Jimmy's, who worked in a firm of property management, suggested that they take over the house and manage it for me at a nominal fee. I was to have "no worries." It made little difference; I found the management little use, and had to employ my invaluable solicitor to keep chasing them! It was like the "caucus" race in *Alice's Adventures in Wonderland*, where they all keep running in a circle and nobody wins. Everyone has a dream and mine would have been to have decorated 26 Upper Fitzwilliam Street in its original Georgian decor and to have lived there. Finally I was forced to sell the house, and was lucky to get a good price. In most stories the landlord is depicted as the tyrant; in my case it was the reverse.

My days were lonely. It did not matter any more if meals were late and a bit of dust gathered. One side of the double bed was empty and so cold. I put pillows on Jimmy's side; the knitted pullover he wore when he was ill I clutched like a teddy bear. Mother's voice perpetually cautioned me, "Don't cry; crying will ruin your eyes." But why shouldn't we cry? I think that if no one cried or mourned their dead, there would be no love in the world.

The first party I was invited to as a widow was a challenge. I had to go on my own and I dreaded it but I bought a new outfit and went. It wasn't so bad. I noticed that a few of the women were unfriendly. Not so their husbands, who plied me with food, drink and friendly conversation. I told myself, come off it; you're suffering from widow's paranoia. But later, when the time came to go home, while retrieving my coat I heard a somewhat intoxicated female voice: "These bloody widows. It's always our husbands who have to ferry them home." I stepped into the hall and faced the raddled blonde and her pot-bellied husband who was standing behind her. I said, "Widows, is it? Just have a care it doesn't happen to you," and walked out, slamming the door. I was so cross, I didn't notice the miles' walk home in the dark. But later I sat on my bed and cried tears of hopelessness.

My children naturally were out a lot of the time leading their own lives. I was glad of that; I didn't want them to sit at home mourning, and Jimmy would have hated that too. One day, travelling on a bus, I was struck by the worst toothache I had ever experienced. It was a left back molar. I couldn't move, it was so bad. After about twenty minutes, the pain went but I felt sick with the fear of its coming back. And it did at three in the morning. There was no swelling and no abscess. I tried to remember all the things Jimmy had told me for dealing with pain. I just took Veganin but when I bent down to put on my shoes, the pain came back. It was so bad I was clinging to the edge of the table, wishing I were dead.

I went to a kindly local dentist, who drilled a hole in the offending tooth and packed it with anaesthetic. But after he had taken an X-ray, there was much whispering and I was referred to a surgeon, who immediately booked me into hospital. There I was given a semi-private ward, good for me then because I needed the company. Even though I was settled, my left jaw hurt in a different way from any previous toothaches. Morning dawned and I was wheeled into the lift and down to theatre. The pale blue-gowned surgeon and his team chorused, "Good luck, Mrs Mooney. Good luck, Mrs Mooney." I vaguely wondered why. No one had ever taken a tooth extraction that seriously before. I awoke to a blinding pain in my jaw. I shouted, "Pain!" and a nurse gave me an injection. After a long drugged sleep, I woke again and lifted up a mirror. I looked as if Cassius Clay had been having a bash at my face; it was all bruised and swollen. Tearfully, I looked in my mouth and saw four black nylon stitches. I could only assume it was some kind of growth in my jaw. I was ten days in hospital and became so thin that they had to stop giving me injections because they hurt too much. It was a long slow haul back to health again.

When I started to feel better, I decided to apply for work as a nurse's aide. I got this position in a home for geriatrics and my only nursing experience had been minding poor Jimmy. The hours were 10 a.m.–2.30 p.m. every day except Sunday, the pay £12 per week (it was 1973). I wore the full uniform and was addressed as Nurse Mooney. Billy and Wendy, now responsible teenagers, had Susan, my invaluable help and dear friend, to cater for them while I was out.

It was quite an experience; geriatrics, with all due respect, are not as lovable as children! The way those old people were treated shocked me. They slept four to a room, the bedclothes were rags, the blankets disgusting, and there was a smell of unwashed bodies. If a priest or doctor was due, a hurried rush was made to change the bedlinen. A nurse's aide is lower than a skivvy, and I was given all the really dirty jobs. My first day I was told to wash six old women, put in their teeth, bring them bed-pans (bed-chairs allowed for those capable of getting out of bed). Matron said, "When you wash them, don't forget the other end." They were mostly incontinent and I was sick several times. Once I was caught smoking by matron in the sluice-room where we had to hose down the worst of the bedding. I got a proper dressing down.

I came to the conclusion that I would never have made it as one of Mother Teresa's nursing sisters. The old people were fussy, agitated and ungrateful. And who am I to blame them? Their meals were awful slop. I wanted to report conditions but I hadn't the guts. One old man kept ringing the bell for his bottle (to urinate). I had to hold the bottle; he professed to have the shakes in his hands. He rang fifteen times between 10 a.m. and 2 p.m. One of the nurses laughingly said, "Mr Stone? He's well able to get up and go himself." He was getting his kicks trying it on with Nurse Mooney. The next day when he rang and slyly said, "My bottle, please, nurse," I said, "You ask for it once more and I'll break it over your head." There was a round of applause from the three other men in the room.

There was a rule of "no bed-pans" on the second floor because none of the patients was over seventy, but the real reason was shortage of staff. An incident occurred on that floor which finished my nursing career. A woman was dying. She had turned an awful blue colour and her breathing was very bad. The poor creature whispered, "Could I have a bed-pan, nurse?" Another nurse came into the room. "No bed-pans allowed. Get her out on to the chair." The cleaning woman intervened, "It's cruel. She's dying." The nurse yanked the poor woman out of the bed, banging her leg against the chair. The cleaner said, "May God forgive you! It's wicked, so it is; you'll break her leg." The nurse's response was, "Be quiet! What ever will Nurse Mooney think of us here!" That old woman died the next day. I looked at her but could not see peace on her face.

There was only one qualified nurse in the whole place for the medications and injections. The rest, me included, were just dressed up as nurses. Sickened, at the end of three weeks I walked out. There isn't much going for the old and unloved. I thought about Jimmy and my father. They both had suffered hard deaths, but at least they were surrounded by people who loved them.

A friend told me of a home for paraplegics. Their condition was the result of polio and accidents, but in most cases of that dreadful drug Thalidomide. The job did not entail nursing, but visiting and chatting with the patients four afternoons a week. It also gave the charge-nurse a rest, and in any emergency I had only to ring the bell.

I went to see the matron, who said, "We would be awfully grateful but I'm wondering if you're strong enough."

"Do you mean physically or mentally?"

She laughed in a kind way. "Physically, my dear. They are all in wheelchairs, and the recreation room has a ramp leading to the garden. It is quite difficult getting the heavier patients up and down." Then she added, "But come in on Monday and we'll see." I suddenly thought of Father. If we ever wanted anything, he never gave a direct answer; he always said, "We'll see."

I reported on a sunny July afternoon for my trial run. A nice nurse spoke to me, "Now before we go in, there are a few things I should tell you. The patients are in recreation from 1.30 to 2.30 to give us a break. Because you are new they will be up to tricks; we've no saints here. You'll find they'll want you to wheel them out to the garden—except Ivor and Ian whom we call the 'chessmen.' You'll see for yourself. Don't wheel them out. At 2.30 the staff will come on and *we'll* do the wheeling. Another thing: some people react badly to them; they are not all a pretty sight. Anyway have a try, and see how you get on."

I felt very apprehensive. My heart was banging. The nurse brought me into a large room full of patients in wheelchairs, introduced me and disappeared. There was an awful silence as every eye focused on me. I decided to walk around and have a word with each of them. A pretty girl smiled at me, "Hallo there, my name is Pat." I noticed that she was covered with a rug. Her feet were where her knees should have been. Later when I got to know her, she told me that her mother had taken Thalidomide. She was twenty-four and, since her parents were both working, she stayed in day-care and was taken home in the evenings. She wanted to go to college, but said it was too difficult. She was doing a postal course in economics and was in no way sorry for herself. I tentatively said, "What about the future?" To my amazement, she said that she would like to get married, adding, "I can have a baby, though my little legs don't work, so I cannot walk." I reckoned she must be tiny. She was exceptionally pretty, with lovely hands.

The drug Thalidomide was recommended for pregnant women: a sedative and hypnotic drug, it appeared to be useful and safe. It came to the United Kingdom in 1958 and was freely used as a tranquilliser. By 1961, Thalidomide was in fact responsible for the birth of a number of deformed children, a terrible tragedy. It was withdrawn in 1961.

Harry was aged about thirty. He had no arms or legs, but he wanted to smoke all the time, despite the fact that he had a horrific cough! There was a packet of cigarettes on the table beside him. "Give me a cig," he said. I put one in his mouth and lit it, noticing that he had no teeth. He sucked in the cigarette until it nearly disappeared. Three times he did this, smoke billowing from his nose. Finally there was a violent paroxysm of coughing and spitting. He had a white handkerchief spread across his chest. "Wipe my chin," he said. I did so, feeling a bit queasy.

I crossed to the bay window where two men were playing chess. I knew it was a slow game, but the "chessmen" had not made a move for half an hour. I stood watching, not daring to speak. Suddenly a bare foot shot across the board and with agile dexterity seized a pawn. I was half asleep, so I nearly collapsed. They were both armless. I looked down at the two pairs of bare feet. The toes looked longer and far more mobile than average. I noticed that those who had the use of their arms all moved their wheelchairs with considerable ease. Someone said, "Wheel me out to the garden," and then there was a chorus of, "We want to go out to the garden." I said to them, "Don't be mean, playing up because I'm new. I know you all go out at 2.30—so nothing doing."

It took a while to get to know them; in fact it was an endurance test. But after a while I became accepted. Finally I was taken for granted, and that is when it became too much for me. Every day I was given endless errand lists: notepaper, stamps, hard-to-get books and magazines. I was rarely paid and was so out of pocket that I had to pack it in. In all fairness, I don't think the nurses knew the demands the patients made on my good nature.

15

TREATMENT BEGINS

When I finally recovered my health and made an effort with my appearance, I started accepting invitations and going about again. I was fifty and I suppose I did not look my age because a few men came my way with strictly dishonourable intentions. It seemed odd going out with other men, although I enjoyed their company, if not their intentions. Widows fall into two categories—the merry and the morose. Society in Ireland is totally twosome orientated. Often if two women friends go out for a drink on their own, people (men) suspect that they are out looking for a man. I never ever had any intention of marrying again. All I wanted was to get enough money together to live on and, with luck, be able to leave something behind me for my three offspring.

Then the nightmare began. It started with agitation. I could not bear to be alone, and would go for long walks which tired me out. Yet even so I could not sleep at night. I started getting attacks of what I can only describe as fear but of what I did not know. My hands would tremble, my heart would pound. I could not stop crying and I did not know what to do or to whom to turn. In desperation, I rang up my nice gynaecologist and he referred me to a psychiatrist. The psychiatrist decided that I needed hospitalisation and so did I. He was worried and, since he was going away on a ten-day break, he gave me tranquillisers and another psychiatrist's phone number, telling me that if I felt worse she would book me in and sedate me.

It was all very ominous but I was too upset to care very much. I could not stop crying and had an overwhelming feeling of sadness and utter helplessness. I had enough wit to go out and buy some nice nightdresses. I was asked would I settle for St John of God, the large psychiatric hospital in Dublin, but it was too far off the beaten track for my family to get to. I personally detest anyone who condemns mental illness. I felt no shame but I have a relative who despised me and never once visited me or even sent a card. In the end I went into a private hospital and was given a room on the third floor—the cuckoo's nest.

"Into bed," said a nurse. "We are going to sedate you rather heavily and you won't know much for five days." Sedated I was; I couldn't even feed myself. I knew what was going on and who was in the room, but I could not help lapsing into sleep. Depression is a horrible illness. No one will ever hear a psychiatrist or psychologist use the words "mad" or "over the top," only "sick" or "ill." I discovered that the two most common types of depression are reactive and endogenous. Reactive is caused by a specific situation: a bereavement, financial stress, marital problems and the like. Endogenous is a recurring depression and is generally thought to be caused by hereditary elements, environment, rejection, or a chemical imbalance in the brain. Offspring of alcoholic parents are sufferers and so I was taken to be endogenous.

After five days of sedation, hopeless tears still ran copiously down my cheeks. Was I crying all these tears for my mother? She said she could not cry, had never cried. Perhaps I was crying for her. A bright nurse came into the room. "No breakfast for you, Mrs Mooney; you're having treatment." I didn't even know what "treatment" meant. That morning, through the haze of sleeping pills, I realised that I was to have the one thing I dreaded and never thought would happen to me: ECT—electroconvulsive therapy—an electric shock through the brain. I had heard and read such horrifying things about it and I became terrified. Unfortunately I had also seen the film *One Flew over the Cuckoo's Nest*. All sorts of notions flew through my fuddled mind. In the film Louise Fletcher strapped down and gagged Jack Nicholson and he was given electric shocks without an anaesthetic. My mind was in a state of helpless panic, like someone going to the electric chair must feel. I heard footsteps in the corridor and something on wheels being trundled along. Bright Nurse, as we called her, bustled in and chirped, "Now, dear, let's get you ready." Another nurse came in. They took the top and bottom off the iron bedstead, and removed the bedclothes, even the pillow.

"Any medals, false teeth, dear?" My psychiatrist, horribly cheerful, was there, and the anaesthetist, a kindly type of man, said, "Lie down, dear, I'm just going to give you an injection in the back of the hand." I felt the pain of the needle, a taste of almonds in my mouth and then nothing. When I awoke, my head felt like a kicked-about football and I had a nasty headache. A nurse gave me a pill for the pain. I was propped up and a breakfast tray was put in front of me. I felt nothing but I'd stopped crying. I ate mechanically. A few visitors came later. I could not remember their names and after they'd gone forgot their visit.

Electroconvulsive treatment is given only in severe cases. I had never contemplated suicide but my state of mind was a feeling of utter hopelessness, and perhaps without treatment I might have actually done it. I must have been very ill because I was in the hospital for twelve weeks. Happily, at the end of my sojourn in hospital my memory was perfect and has remained so, leaving me wondering am I the exception that confirms the rule. I had no worries about home because Susan, my home help and friend, looked after the family in my absence. Eventually I was allowed out to browse around the local shops and sometimes a friend took me out for a day. I had no tears left but I was full of pills and all the time felt detached and very sad.

Finally, I was allowed to go home. But even in that short time I had become institutionalised and I did not like being at home. There was an emptiness to try and fill in. The children were adults now and scarcely ever around. The nest was empty! Sadly I was never at home long enough to feel settled. For the five years after my breakdown I was hospitalised twice or three times a year, and never for less than ten weeks. My suitcase was always packed. Looking back, I often wonder how I survived the medication; several times I had bad side-effects from the many pills. The worst was when I hallucinated and thought there was a horse in the wardrobe. This luckily happened in the hospital. I believed I heard him kicking. It was terrifying! Another set of pills brought me out in red spots. All medication has side-effects, yet there seems to be no other way. Sometimes I wonder morbidly what the inside of my head must be like. I have had so much shock treatment I cannot help feeling there is something terrible about it.

While I was in hospital I was allowed to walk the corridors. I remember a man who used to march up and down for hours. At the end of the corridor he would do a military about turn. He never spoke; his eyes were the eyes of a man on a route march. A young priest in the room next to mine sent me in a present carefully wrapped. I eagerly opened it. It was a tooth he had had extracted, a revolting long fang! I felt sick. But the other patients were kind, helpful and intelligent. It is usually sensitive and intelligent people who suffer from depression. I suppose it's like being an alcoholic, where the drink controls the person. Mine kept coming back. Sometimes it got so bad I almost liked going back into hospital. There I was in a twilight zone of drugs. Nothing was expected of me and I felt almost secure. I was back again for the fourth, fifth, or sixth time; I didn't know, didn't care. The nice bouncy nurse would meet me as the lift stopped at the third floor— the psychiatric wing. "Hullo dear, welcome back. You have the same room overlooking the garden. They're all here, all your friends. Miss Brophy's still in her room."

Miss Brophy lived in the ward. She was a senile geriatric,

about ninety, who just sat in her chair all day looking at television. She stared into the screen even when it was on the blink, every now and then calling out, "Nurse, nurse, nurse!" over and over. Mass was said in her room for her ninetieth birthday. There were flowers and cards. Her room was crowded with people. I looked at the old woman packed into her chair. She was oblivious to all of it, her eyes vacant. Later there was a cake, candles, people saying, "Happy birthday, happy birthday." Did the nurse think it was some kind of bonus for us all to be there?

Patients were not allowed to lock any doors, and that included the bathroom and the lavatory. I found it disconcerting. Once I was having a bath when a male patient walked in; lavatory and bath were *en suite*. He proceeded to spend a penny, while I crouched so low in the bath that I nearly drowned. He flushed the toilet and then, looking right into the bath, said, "What are you doing in the Gents?" I yelled at him, "Get out! Get out! I'll ring the alarm bell if you don't." He replied, "If you think I get a turn on from looking at a miserable-looking old one like a boiling fowl, you're making a mistake." He banged the door as he went out.

On my way back to my bedroom, Mary, a friend who was also being treated for depression, called me. "Come quick, I've something to show you." A room marked Private, which was usually kept locked, was open. Mary told me that all the stuff they used on us for ECT was in there. I said, "I don't want to see it."

John the porter said we should know what they were doing to us. Morbid curiosity got the better of me, especially since the No-Breakfast sign was on my door. That meant treatment in the morning. There was a tall thing on wheels with a bag and mask. That was the oxygen. It was what I used listen to as it trundled down the corridor. The "shock box" looked like a radar direction-finder machine, all buttons and stops; there were headphones that plugged into it and a voltage switch. Mary had the procedure off pat: "What actually happens is, after the anaesthetic is given in the back of the hand, you get a second injection that paralyses the body's muscles so that when the electric current is passed through the head, it doesn't cause strong muscular convulsions or contractions through the body."

After Miss Brophy's party I wrote in my little book of memoirs: "How sad that here I am secure; it's almost like going home. The dope will be around soon and there will be no more of that bloody thinking—not for weeks." The nurse prattled on while she made up the bed. "Isn't it nice to have your old room?" I undressed, climbed into the high hospital bed, and thought, "Here goes the old routine: into bed, eat, sleep, wash, swallow pills."

Even the shock box was welcome because the Pentothal knocked me out for a while. Later, we of the third floor would gradually conform to our pattern. We would come out of heavy sedation after five days. Still doped, we would wander along the corridors, in and out of each other's rooms; we formed friendships and had heart-to-heart talks; we would discuss the terrible food and that bitch of a nurse we all hated. She was a sadist and seemed to enjoy giving us injections. We all have an innate loyalty to our doctors: "we depend on them you see." The outside world was rarely mentioned; it is a frightening place. It's all right in here. We didn't have to make decisions. We would talk about our visitors, but those out there don't relate to us; we relate only to each other. I used to think: is this where I really belong?

For ECT a headset with sticky pads is adjusted on each side of the temples. In early days the convulsions were so strong that bones were broken. Nowadays, we're told, the patient merely twitches. The anaesthetist pumps air into the lungs while the muscles are paralysed (this includes the breathing muscles). As soon as the paralysing drug's effect has been reversed, another injection is made and normal breathing returns. It is supposed to take only about three minutes. I do not understand ECT but it worked for me. Initially I did feel better. But I also felt that it was immoral to do such things to the human brain; it's like plugging it into the mains. I did once have a rather scary thought: perhaps one suffered at the time of shocks and forgot afterwards.

Anti-depressive drugs and ECT went on for five awful years. The psychiatrist who had looked after me all that time died in July 1979. For patients this can be very traumatic because we have this dependency, and it is very difficult starting all over again with a new doctor. Here, for the record, I must add that I was lucky. My new psychiatrist is splendid, and without that doctor's encouragement and belief in me, my two books would not have been written. I have always said that there isn't much difference between good honest confessions and psychiatric sessions, albeit the penances are slightly different! The humiliation of baring the soul is the same; so, paradoxically, is the relief. I don't know how or why, but I got better. My last time to be hospitalised was May 1979. I will always carry the label "endogenous" but now I have learned to live with it and know that attacks too will pass.

16

BABYLON REVISITED

Since my father died before Pauline was a year old, the following incident strikes me as strange and a little sad. When Pauline was three years old she suddenly started wanting to go to bed early. At six-thirty, after tea, she would say, "Can I go to bed now?" I thought it was because she wanted to talk to her collection of dolls. She would put them on the bed and, in the manner of little children, talk to them. It amused me to listen to her prattling away. One evening she said as usual, "Ma, Ma, can I go to bed now?" I said, "Oh, but it's so early. Tell me why do you want to go up to bed?" Pauline said, "I want to see that nice old man."

"What old man? What do you mean?"

"He comes and sits beside me on the chair. He doesn't talk but he smiles and he listens to me."

"What does he look like?"

"He's got white hair and has a red dressing gown with gold writing on the pocket." She gave me an exact description of my father. It seems that he was coming back to visit the little granddaughter he had never really known.

I used to hear her talking to him. When I asked her: "Does he talk to you?" she replied, "He doesn't talk, ma-ma, but I know what he is saying." The visitations lasted about three weeks. Then Pauline reverted to form and wanted to stay up as late as possible. Her grandfather had paid his last visit.

It is a momentous thing to sell one's home. My doctor seriously advised me to move. To anyone who has recently lost a partner, my advice is: "Don't!", unless your financial situation is such that you have to go. I had brought up our children in our little house and we had lived our twenty-three years of marriage there. I do not believe all that can happen without leaving something of us behind, especially in a house where children have grown from babies into adults, where I loved and listened with acute awareness to the things my three children told me. There were birthday parties, new babies, the first tooth, all the long road of mumps, measles, whooping coughs, the heartbreak of having to send the children to school for the first time, the selfless love our seventeen-year-old son showed in helping me nurse his dying father. When, finally, the For Sale notice went up, there was that distressing invasion of privacy: house opened for viewing, people who had no intention of buying opening cupboards, making remarks like "I don't like the colour of that room; I'd take that built-in seat out and put my sofa there," as if the woman already owned the house. One man even got up on the roof to inspect it! I felt like someone forced to walk through the foyer of a crowded hotel stark naked!

Finally, the house was sold. I was content because nice people bought it. Because there was no one to advise me, I was conned. I was told that there was not enough in the house for an auction. Except for basic essentials, my antique furniture (from Saintbury), some priceless wall-plates, silver, good china—all were sold for a thousand pounds to a dealer. At the time I was taken advantage of. I was not well and was on Valium. Later, when I got better, I was very upset at my loss.

I had bought an apartment in Sandycove, near the sea. The morning came when we were all packed and ready to leave Dundela Park. I remember sitting in the little breakfast room drinking the last cup of coffee. The furniture removal van was parked outside the gate. One of the workmen called me aside and said, "We are about to move off. Would you go into your sitting-room for a few minutes on your own and then walk out of the house before we move the chairs. Walk out and don't look back." That man knew I had to say my good-byes and seeing the worn and used chairs going was all part of the heartache. I did what he said and didn't look back. As far as my apartment goes, it is still anonymous—just a place to hang your hat. I won't ever have a home again.

My actress sister, Maureen O'Sullivan, invited my daughter Wendy and me to New York for three weeks in 1978. I had seen very little of Maureen over the years but we had kept in touch by letter. The last time I went to the US was with Mother in 1938. We went in October, in what the North Americans call the fall. Luckily we had sunshine every day.

Maureen's apartment overlooked Central Park and the lake. It was like a large piece of country transplanted into the middle of grimy old New York. Maureen once lived there on her own. When she married James Cushing, her daughter Mia took over the spacious apartment to live there with her eleven children, four of her own and seven adopted. The apartment was pleasant. But I remembered the time when she and her husband, the late John Farrow, shared a Spanish-style house with a swimming-pool in fashionable Bel-Air. Bougainvillea climbed the balconies and at night the crickets sang and the air was fragrant with magnolia and gardenias.

When we arrived in New York Maureen announced very firmly, "I don't cook, so you have to eat out." Wendy and I slept in her library on a pull-out convertible bed that doubled as a settee. The hall was full of lovely mirrors embossed with ivy leaves; it was annoying because you couldn't see into them. Behind the mirrors were cupboards where we hung our clothes. There were no curtains on the windows but we were given sleep masks; they took a while to get used to. I wondered how our postman in Ireland would take it, if I blundered to the door wearing my mask. Everyone cut up their food, and then ate it with their forks. Maureen berated me for going to the hairdressers. "Only old ladies go to the hairdressers here." I hadn't her thick curls, and could not manage mine. She went for a manicure every week and coloured her own hair.

I brought no smart clothes; the only expensive item I had was a green velvet jacket. Everything else was from Dunnes Stores and I was not in the least bit worried.

Regarding the hair, I noticed that most of Maureen's actress friends looked a bit of a mess.

One day I picked up a small silver cigarette box, embossed with the words, "To Maureen, love Frank."

"Sinatra, wouldn't you know! He can be careful with his money!" said Maureen. I asked what he was really like. "He can be charming, is a wonderful host, runs a marvellous house, and nothing is forgotten for his guests!" said his ex-mother-in-law. Mia is a wonderful mother who makes two films a year, because, as she says herself, "I need the money for the kids."

Sadly while Wendy and I were in New York we did not meet Mia, who was then living in California. All we managed was a chat over the telephone. Wendy and I were quite happy to explore New York on our own. Everywhere we went, as soon as it was discovered that we were Irish, we were offered free drinks and a great welcome. We discovered an Irish bar, and got talking to three charming Irishmen. We didn't find out until later that they were members of Provisional IRA and wanted men. They stood us drinks and were very good company. One, a tall thin man, was to my way of thinking quietly intellectual; the second was a tough fat man who looked like a building labourer, and the third was a smooth-talking, good-looking fellow—an obvious con-man, I thought to myself. Without going into any detail the fat man confided, "We're all with the lads," and said he was just out of prison. The smoothie said, "I am on the run." The intellectual was reticent and did not talk so much. I had always had a morbid interest in what active members of the IRA are like. I discovered what I should have realised; they are ordinary people like the rest of us.

It was a Sunday and they were all going to mass. They wanted us to go too and then have lunch or American brunch (breakfast-cum-lunch) with them. We declined. When I discovered their secret, I left the bar rather hurriedly. One of them, the fat man, ran down the road after us, puffing, badly out of breath. He panted, "Take these in memory of your visit—and God bless." He gave me four lovely opals.

Everywhere of social importance we went, I wore what I came to call my uniform. (Maureen would diplomatically say, "I think understated elegance.") That was: my green velvet jacket, a tweed skirt, pearls borrowed from Maureen and a good handbag. I was broke and the rest of my clothes were not quite *comme il faut* for wearing to glitterati parties. Sometimes I felt drab. At one party we went to I needed two gins to drown my inhibitions. We had been invited by Arnold Weissburger and Hilton Goldman (as rich as their names) for "cocktails" on the occasion of veteran actress Helen Hayes's birthday. She had been born in 1896, played Amanda in Tennessee Williams's play *The Glass Menagerie* and founded in the mid-sixties the HH Repertory Company which specialised in Shakespeare readings. Helen Hayes was receiving guests in the company of her lifelong friend Lillian Gish, who had been born in the same year and starred in *Birth of a Nation* and *Intolerance*. When we arrived, a lively man bellowed out our names and we were welcomed by Messrs Weissburger and Goldman and immediately introduced to the two actresses. Helen Hayes was a very nice old lady, but Lillian Gish, unlike Helen, had retained her beauty—not the beauty of youth but of a Dresden quality of feature. She had silver hair and a silver dress, the only colour being a large pink rose on her shoulder.

My impression was that everything and everyone glittered! Lighted chandeliers, shimmering gowns, blazing jewellery. Maureen disappeared and I was left on my own in my governess outfit. The best thing to do? I downed rather quickly two gin-and-tonics. As I glanced round the crowded room, I was conscious of how very different from a Dublin party it was; even the noise was different with loud American accents. The scent from so much expensive perfume was overpowering—but at least no one smoked. I spotted film stars whom I had met just before the war on my first trip to Hollywood when I was eighteen. They were still recognisable but as one came in closer they looked like exhibits in a wax museum—pale, lightly painted skins, bright capped teeth, tired old eyes and wrinkled hands clutching bejewelled bags. I started to study those hands and they all seemed tense—what face-lift can add one day to the span of a person's life. The men were just as bad with their tints and toupee tucks. I bravely made my way over to Joan Fontaine, still a beautiful woman. I enjoyed meeting Jean Marsh who helped devise the famous television series *Upstairs Downstairs*, and played Grace the prim parlourmaid. She looked quite different, with long blonde hair, a mini skirt and a black sweater with her name Jean inscribed in diamanté. She told me that she had not been asked out for three months, and she was lonely always sitting in. She said that it was the price of fame:

people think you're too rich, too stuck up, especially men—they shy off. Strange to hear that from a glamorous television star.

A nice-looking, very young man came up to me and said, "You're Maureen's sister. I have just married an Irish girl; will you come and meet her?" I assented. Someone intervened the young man said, "Go meet her; she's in the adjoining room. I'll join you in a minute."

I said, "But how will I know her?"

"You'll know her—anyone can spot an Irish girl."

I walked into the equally large adjoining room. I could not spot any female who looked like an Irish girl. Finally the young man found me. "What! You've not found her yet!" He propelled me across the room. "Roisín, here's Maureen's sister." I was facing a very fat, white-haired woman, well into her forties. She was proudly displaying her solitaire and wore a corsage of red carnations. She could have passed for his mother. I was told later that she had money, lots of it. Irish girl how are you! I turned to say hello to a very colourful lady who seemed familiar. She said, "Hi! I'm Ginger." I didn't like to say, "Are you Ginger Rogers?" though she did have a resemblance to her. Her face was so stretched that she could barely smile, her bosom uplifted enough so that you could balance a cup and saucer on it. This bright blonde with old hands whispered to me, "Darling, I haven't my specs. Would you look in my glass? I'm either very drunk or there's a large spider swimming in my gin fizz." I looked at her and noticed that one of her eyes looked funny. Then I realised that one eye was decorated with long eyelashes, the other one bald because the lashes had fallen into her drink! I told her. "Oh my Gawd!" She fished it out with red talon fingernails. "Powder room calling, darling." And off she went.

That night going back to Maureen's apartment in Central Park Square, I saw a man huddled up beside the steps asleep, his only covering a tattered coat. I asked the Spanish doorman, who said, "He stay there, missie, two, three days. They come and take him away." It was October and cold. Inside the block lived rich people all nice and warm. I didn't sleep that night. My mind frequently went back to the days of long ago, to gentle holidays in the Roscommon countryside, where the brown water sparkled as it wove its way down to the dark woods. Silence and dappled sunlight would never meet this concrete jungle. The old houses that never knew radio or television, electric light or telephones, never missed those things, for then there was time for conversation, for music and a gentle way of living and thinking. In New York I felt like a ghost walking about in a world full of things and people I didn't like.

Maureen had an elderly millionaire friend. He had bought a three-storey luxury apartment from a famous actress. Wendy and I were invited there to a formal dinner. Strangely, everything was very proper but the food was terrible. The set-up in this man's house was thus: he was looked after by a Filipino couple, the man a factotum, valet and chauffeur, the woman cook and housekeeper. The couple had an eleven-year-old daughter, Lili. The old man had legally adopted her and she was heir to all his money. To see this very mature child sitting at the dinner-table while her own father and mother waited on her was bizarre.

Maureen decided to throw a farewell party for Wendy and myself. We had no friends in New York, so had to leave it to her to send invitations. I mentioned that Maureen hates cooking—so she doesn't cook; she hates washing up—so she doesn't wash up. Disposable cups, plates and cutlery were bought. Mother would have had a fit.

The guest-list consisted of some old escorts of my sister; Milo and Kitty O'Shea (though he hardly spoke the whole evening); the veteran actor John Beal and his wife; the old millionaire and his parish priest, who walked three paces behind him like Uriah Heep; a few young people who played records and smoked joints in an adjoining room. Maureen's friend Leonora, a dramatic type in floaty chiffon, kept saying, "Look at those darling little Irish people." I was very aware of the difference between an Irish party and an American one. The same large amount of drink was lowered, but, as actors will, the guests talked and talked about themselves, and the "wit" was missing. No one opened the piano or sang a bit of a song.

The preparation of the food was really something. Wendy boiled up pounds and pounds of minced meat and put just about every vegetable into the pot. She decorated each helping with mashed potato and chopped parsley. It passed as a "darling Irish recipe." Everyone was mad for it.

Maureen had thought that she, for once, would bake a ham. No one was allowed into the kitchen. I took a peep; the ham, coated in brown sugar and beautifully scored and dotted with cloves, stood at the ready. One hour later I heard Maureen's shrieks. The ham, baked in a hot oven, was coal-black and solidified. However, we took a hammer and chisel to it and found that the inside was edible—so what the eye don't see the heart don't grieve for.

Departure day arrived. Wendy and I were hardly up and dressed before Maureen was dismantling the bed and putting everything in order again. It was as if she were shaking off the dust of our visit. Some years later my wish for her came true, when at Saratoga races she met James Cushing. They are married and living happily ever after.

17

LIFE GOES ON

I moved to the Sandycove apartment, into anonymity. I was lucky that Billy and Wendy were still with me. Pauline married David, a scotsman, and lived in England, the first chick to leave the nest.

My cousin Betty Frazer had none of the flamboyance of the Frazer clan, but her anecdotes about that bizarre family were very amusing. One of them I thought particularly funny since it involved Maureen. Two years ago the Maureen O'Sullivan Fan Club in Boyle invited her to visit them and stay in our grandfather's ancestral home, Riversdale Lodge. There was a parade with pipes through the town, with Maureen in an open landau. They stopped at the house in the main street where she was born in 1911 over a Miss Judd's haberdashery. A plaque on the wall commemorates the occasion. Since the family were such snobs, I have always wondered why the birthplace was so humble. The grandparents and grand-aunts lived in their stately homes. My father was then living on a captain's pay and perhaps he was proud. Anyway Grandmother Frazer was always nasty about him because the O'Sullivans had been merchants in County Cork and she looked down on trade but suffered it because the O'Sullivans would one day be rich, when their wealthy guardian, who lived in London, died. He did eventually leave everything to my father.

On Maureen's visit one of her duties was to plant a tree in the grounds of Riversdale Lodge, which is now a hotel. She planted a monkey-puzzle tree. Betty Frazer told me that Grandfather, who was a highly superstitious spiritualist, had a horror of trees. He said they were unlucky and would not have them in the grounds. Yet here was his grand-daughter planting a tree in remembrance.

Poor Betty has since died. On Boxing Day 1991 a concerned friend called to visit her and found her very confused, obviously ill, though up and dressed. She drove her into hospital there and then. The following day I got word that she was very ill. When I went to the hospital she had been moved from the ward to a small room off it. She was dying. It was incongruous to see this sun-tanned, muscular woman, younger than the rest of us, dying. I clasped her hand and spoke. There was no response. A nurse said, "She was conscious this morning." Beside her bed was a get-well card and a bottle of Kia Ora. I said as the nurses were turning her, "How sad to have no one to care, to die alone,"—and then I felt a most wonderful aura of peace as if an angel was in the room. I said to the pretty dark-haired nurse, "But she definitely is not alone."

"No," she said, "she isn't alone." Everything in that sparse room was white, walls, bedding, even the white hospital gown she wore. I looked at her workworn hands. She had lived a lonely life. Death is the time when the spirit becomes manifest. There was sunshine. She looked not beautiful but radiant. My personal belief is that radiance comes only from the spirit. And so she died and, in all her aloneness, in the white room and the pale sunlight these words came very clearly to me: "Be still, and know that I am God."

The hospital authorities were so taken aback at her death that they asked my permission for an autopsy. She had had septicaemia and they had tried every drug but she had responded to none. After a service in the local Protestant church, her remains were taken to Roscommon to the Frazer burial ground.

I am not a fatalist, but I believe our free will entitles us to do with our lives what we will. Five friends of mine took their own lives, three by drowning and two by drug overdose. Whatever the reasons, they did not want to live any more. I had a close friend—I will call her Julia, not her real name—who had a brute of a husband who hit her when he felt like it, which was fairly often. She loved him but told me that he beat his three boys and terrorised his three daughters. Naturally the children left home as soon as they could. So Julia was left alone with her husband who could be, when he felt like it, a charming and amusing man. One night she phoned me, "I've done it, I've taken another overdose." Luckily their house was near, so I ran over. The back door was open, Julia was lying on a chair in the sitting-room, half conscious. I took one look and dialled for an ambulance. Her arm looked broken and her face had a nasty bruise. I will always be in awe of the expertise and kindness of the ambulance team. I went with her, the sirens screaming. In casualty she was put on a table. It took at least four people to hold her down. She had regained consciousness and was fighting and thrashing about. A young doctor swished back the curtain and asked me, "What's her name? Do you know what she took?" I handed him the two bottles I had found beside her— Demerol and Lithium. Soon I could hear, "Come on now, Julia. Open your mouth." They were pumping her out. I kept my hands over my ears. Finally they appeared, with Julia on a trolley, white and unconscious: "We're taking her up to intensive care. Will you try and inform her husband?"

"Will she be all right?" I asked.

"We won't know till morning." After phoning numerous pubs, I located her husband, told him where she was and banged down the phone.

Well, they saved Julia's life. I saw her the following afternoon. "Look at me!" She fumbled in her bag for a mirror. "Lazarus back from the dead, that's what I am; back from the dead." I looked at her skinny arms, one partly bandaged; it hadn't been broken, just dislocated. The ward smelled of stale old women, lavender water, urine. An old black-robed nun parted the curtains, "Father's coming. Get prepared for confession." Julia gave her the fingers sign, behind her back of course. "I'd better get out if you're going to confession," I whispered. We could hear his reverence in with the occupant of the other bed. Swish, and Julia's bed curtains were pulled back. The priest was old, shabby but kindly looking. I left them and sat in the corridor.

Her description of the business afterwards was hilarious, and in no way am I trying to jeer at a kind old priest doing his job. He had sat on the one hard chair and said, "Well now, are you sorry for what you did? Wasn't it a foolish thing, a foolish thing to do, child?" She was tired, so she just said what he wanted her to say: "Yes, Father," while her inner voice was saying, "Go away and leave me in peace." Perspiration was breaking out on his beefy face. He fumbled in the pocket of his black coat, wiped his face in his handkerchief and then slung a violet-coloured ribbon round his neck. Julia said he looked very determined. He came and sat on the bed. "You've got to be sorry. God gave you the precious gift of life. What you tried to do was bad but He'll forgive you..."

Silence, more perspiration. "You've got to be sorry about something." She wanted to say she was sorry to be alive but she was tired and his reverence was sitting on her feet. "I'm sorry if my kids are worried." At this the priest sprang to his feet crying, "That will do; that will do!" a radiant beam upon his face. He raised his hand and intoned, "*Ego te absolvo in nomine Patris, et Filii et Spiritus Sancti. Amen.*" With that he was gone. He passed me sitting on my chair in the corridor. I said, "Hello, Father." He replied absently, "God bless you, child," and shuffled off down the long corridor, his pocket torn, sunlight from an open window shining on his white hair.

It's all been said before but it's worth repeating: the loneliness of widowhood is appalling. Of course the age of the widow is pertinent. Young ones when the worst is over can step on to the roundabout again. Those in their fifties have to turn to other widows. It is very hard to have a social life. I had a friend called Carol who has since died. We were widowed about the same time and since she had a car, we went out for a bit together. One night we thought we'd go to a singles club—just for the crack. I'd done a bit of research and it hadn't taken long to find out that they were full of married men. The clubs on the south-side of Dublin got the boyos from the north-side and vice versa. Carol and I went to our local club. It was a laugh. We sat in the car and watched the men go in. Most of them were in their fifties and some were even older. They carried their dancing shoes in brown paper bags. These were made of patent leather and showed inevitable wear and tear—like the owners, they'd seen better days!

Inside there was a bar full of men tanking up to give themselves Dutch courage. The ladies room was full of middle-aged women. They jostled for a view of the spotty mirror, all in good clothes: floral frocks and silver dance shoes. We walked into the Ballroom of Romance, which was dimly lit and full of plastic palms. The shaded lights and the booze made us all look and feel younger. Canned nostalgic music reverberated and a fat man in a brown suit kept shouting, "The next dance will be a Paul Jones." No one took any notice. The women sat at the tables round the dance floor pretending not to notice the men. In no time my friend was whisked away by a little fox-trotting salesman, wearing a toupee and black patent dancing shoes. I was pursued by a big hunk who towered over me. After all, I am only five feet tall. It was embarrassing to find myself gripped under the armpit, and to listen to his clumsy come-on: "Aren't you grand now! Do you ever go for a drink or a bit of a walk?" I decided that it was not for me. I'd rather stay at home and read a good book.

Then one day a friend showed me an item in the evening paper. Brian Cleeve, the writer, had announced that he was working on a book about loneliness and wanted to hear from readers about their experiences. I sent him some of the material I had written and he was delighted. I was naturally pleased when he suggested that my memories could be made into a good book. I met Brian and he is now a good friend, as indeed is his charming wife, Veronica. Because I was still insecure, I sent efforts to several other famous writers, including John B Keane, who wrote me a wonderful letter. He said, "It's time you saw an editor. Your writing has power and all the makings of a lucrative and readable book." If you read this, John B, it's saying, "Thank you so very much."

I started writing in earnest. Strangely, when I had finished, the first thought that came into my head was that if my book were ever published I would go to Mother's grave and leave a big bunch of plastic roses. She loved artificial flowers, especially the roses. She was a law unto herself.

I called my book *A Strange Kind of Loving* and Mother was the star of the story. Poolbeg Press published it. It was a bestseller and there were radio and television interviews. The night before my first live television appearance, I dreamed of Mother. She was in Saintbury. When we lived there we had a big cow bell which she used as a dinner-gong. She used bang it when meals were ready and since Father was almost always somewhere in the garden she would stand outside the hall door and as she rang the heavy bell would chant, "Charlie, Charlie, Charlie!" He hated being called that, as do most men whose name is Charles. Anyway, there she was in my dream ringing the bell and calling his name very loudly, and then she changed the name to mine and shouted, "Sheila, Sheila, Sheila." I think she knew about the book—that first book, the story of the first part of my life.

The Man Above always gives something in recompense for sorrow. For me, it was the birth of my darling little grandson, Oisin, my younger daughter's son and my only grandchild. I used not want to be old. Now I pray I'll be allowed some time to watch my grandson grow up a little. I often think the relationship between grandparents and grandchildren is so very special because usually it's not a very long one and so much love has to be packed into a limited span.

The week that *A Strange Kind of Loving* was published, I went on my promised visit to Mother's grave. It is in a very large cemetery, with a vast expanse of graves. I never know where her grave is but the strange thing is that I have only to stand inside the main gates and something directs me. Like a robot I walk for fifteen minutes, then stop in front of the grave.

That day was sunny. I walked in the dappled light between the yew trees, standing ever silent sentinels. Mother's words came back to me. She was always repeating "resting where no shadows fall." I was carrying a bunch of plastic roses, big with long stems. She always said she preferred them to real flowers. As before, I walked directly to her grave. I stood contemplating the headstone and surround. She had died the way she wanted: in her sleep in the cold grey hours of dawn. I felt tears prickling the back of my eyes and fancied I heard her words again: "Don't cry—it ruins one's eyes." I blew my nose and started to try and arrange the plastic roses in sun-baked soil.

Someone spoke behind me. It was Ned, one of the keepers. He was carrying two flower containers, those things full of holes. "That won't work. The ground is like cement. These were thrown on the dump. This one's not bad." He offered me an excellent white container and I thanked him. I thought, what a strange coincidence. Mother's life was full of strange coincidences. I arranged the plastic roses. They looked rather gay. Ned had known Mother. He said, "Why, Missus, with all the lovely flowers, did you bring the likes of them?"

"They were her choice, not mine," I replied. He tipped his cap to me and then to the grave: "May God be good to her." Does she know I'm here, I wondered. I know the Christian belief is that the soul has gone on. Even so, I get a feeling that those who have passed over are aware of us and pleased that we recall them. I remembered her portraits. They were good because you always felt the personality of the sitter, the strength of character. This was especially pertinent because she always painted them faceless, saying, "You have to imagine the face." I never found that hard.

She was, as she so often said, a law unto herself. I stood back and looked at her grave. I didn't say good-bye. We never said good-bye even when she died. I headed for the main gates.

Also By

Sheila Mooney

A Strange Kind of Loving

A bittersweet memoir of an Ascendancy
upbringing

POOLBEG